Empower your voice.

Digital Assistants

Digital Assistants

TESOL Strategy Guide

DAVID KENT

Pedagogy Press

A catalogue record for this book is available from the National Library of Australia

ISBN: 9781925555417

Pedagogy Press. Sydney, Australia.
www.pedagogypress.com

First Edition.

For teachers everywhere.

CONTENTS

Preface

This *TESOL Strategy Guide*, number seven in the set, arose out of the clear need to provide teacher training and a means of professional development to educators who are living and working in the Republic of Korea. Many expatriate English language instructors have arrived in-country without training as a teacher or educator, and are often left to take care of their own professional development while engaged in teaching English to speakers of other languages (TESOL). As many of these teachers come to enjoy working as expatriates, they often begin to seek out their own professional development on topics that they wish to learn more about, on skills that they wish to gain, and on techniques that they wish to integrate within their classrooms. It is this need, which is common to all teachers of English in all contexts around the globe, that this book seeks to fill.

Organization of the text
Each *TESOL Strategy Guide* can be read standalone or in conjunction with others from the set. Each book provides information on a technology topic, and has been designed around a question-based format similar to the following:

- Overview
- What is … ?
- How can I use … ?
- What types of … exist?
- What elements are behind an effective … ?
- How can … lend itself to TESOL?
- How can I start using … with students?
- How do I evaluate a … ?
- What tools are available for … creation?
- How do I craft a … ?
- How would I use a tool to create a … ?
- What are the key points behind … use in the TESOL context?

A comprehensive list of resources with links to pertinent websites and applications is included along with lesson plan guides, example implementation techniques, and various free-to-use handouts for the teacher and student alike. A reference list of all works cited also allows those teachers with an interest in a particular topic to engage in reading further on the issues that most interest them and impact their learners.

It is hoped that this book will provide both education and something new for all teachers – be they trained or untrained, pre-service, in-service, seasoned, or retired.

1
Overview

The fourth industrial revolution has seen the convergence of innovation and technology, led by AI (artificial intelligence), big data, and IoT (the internet of things), and it has restructured industry across all sectors including that of education. These changes have been disruptive, and include how our students interact with us as teachers as well as how we as teachers prepare and provide learning opportunities in and outside of the classroom transform. Moving forward these changes will also see the need to provide learners with different skill sets, not only ones they will need to use to function in the classroom, but in society and the workplace as well. For teachers too, it may also lead to changes regarding with 'whom' we will teach, and how best we might begin to integrate robots and AI-based digital assistants into the classroom as teaching aids, and how their value can be harnessed to provide learners with life-long study companions.

2
What are digital assistants?

Digital assistants, AI (Artificial Intelligence) assistants, or virtual assistants are all names for similar means of supporting a natural way of interacting with machines, each other, and the world around us. They are software-based agents that are able to perform a variety of tasks or services for individuals. They may be run as independent applications or they may be housed in a smart speaker, and although they can work using a variety of interfaces, the most popular is that of a VUI (voice-user interface). In this way, digital assistants are being used to implement a more natural means of interaction between man and machine while also providing increased accessibility options, especially for those with visual impairments. To date, digital assistants are being used for variety of things including: the control of home automation (lights, heating/cooling); retrieval of real-time data (news, weather, stocks, commute information) and general information; the reading of audiobooks; the streaming of music and video; calendar, shopping, reminders, and to-do lists; texting, and making phone calls, and booking reservations on your behalf; searching and purchasing of products (including food) and the tracking of their delivery. Answering general questions was found to be the most predominant use case for digital assistants by the general population of the United States of America, followed by weather information, and the streaming of music (see figure 1).

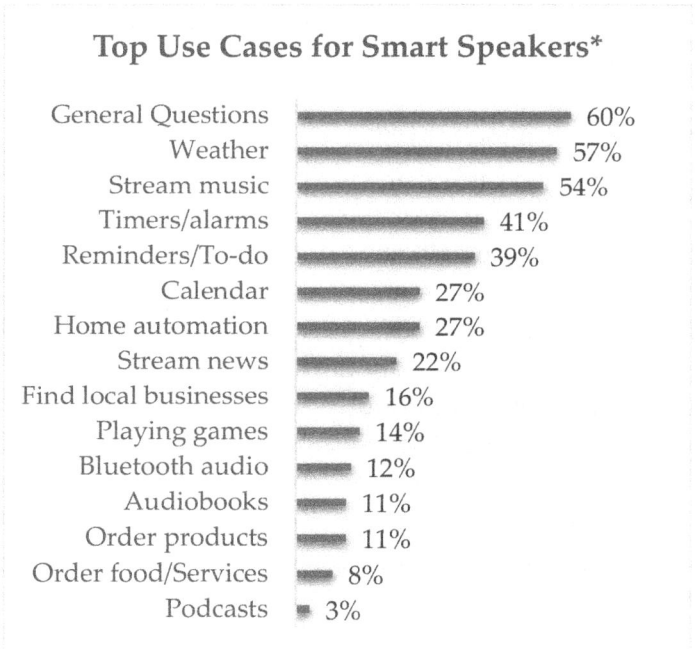

Top Use Cases for Smart Speakers*

Use Case	Percentage
General Questions	60%
Weather	57%
Stream music	54%
Timers/alarms	41%
Reminders/To-do	39%
Calendar	27%
Home automation	27%
Stream news	22%
Find local businesses	16%
Playing games	14%
Bluetooth audio	12%
Audiobooks	11%
Order products	11%
Order food/Services	8%
Podcasts	3%

Figure 1.
Top use cases for Smart Speakers (Marketing Charts, 2017).
* based on a Custom Survey of US Households.

The same interaction that digital assistants provide has long been seen in terms of chatbot use. In 1966, the chatbot Eliza was created at the MIT AI Laboratories to simulate human conversation. It presented the illusion of understanding by matching user prompts to scripted responses (pattern matching), but it had no built-in framework for the contextualization of events. Since then there have been many chatbots, created for many different purposes, two of interest are ALICE and Watson. ALICE (artificial linguistic internet computer entity) is a natural language processing chatbot which relies upon heuristic pattern matching rules when receiving human input (AbuShawar & Atwell, 2015). Watson, developed by IBM, was originally designed to compete on the television show Jeopardy! in which it went on to beat two of the show's former champions (Sony Pictures Television, 2010), and has since gone on to be used to help analyze big data. More recently, messenger bots have been used to engage people using text-based messenger applications, such as Facebook Messenger, for a variety of purposes including that of promoting television series such as Humans (Facebook Business, 2018) or for customer service inquiries. Evidence also suggests that increasing amounts of social media content is being generated by autonomous entities like social bots that interact both with each other and with humans. (Varol et al., 2017). It will only be a matter of time before chatbots, social bots, and digital assistants come to consistently pass the Turing Test (Turing, 1950) where an intelligent machine is indistinguishable from a human during a text-only conversation. The conversation in this test is limited to text-only so that there is no reliance on a verbal rendering component. In fact, the Google Assistant has been seen to verbally pass the Turing test on at least one occasion when it was asked to make a phone call and to book a hair appointment (Welch, 2018).

Overall, in the TESOL context, chatbots have been found to be viewed favorably by learners, with voice-based chatbots better received, and proven more effective than text-based ones, especially for providing teaching and learning in the classroom context (Kim, 2017). It has also long been known that those students who possess low self-confidence in their foreign language abilities do prefer to interact with a chatbot over a human (Fryer, 2006). However, there have also been instances where benefit has been determined to derive from a novelty effect (Fryer et al., 2017), or where chatbot interactions have come to confound communication (chatbot-student) by veering off topic, or where instances of miscommunication (student-chatbot) have occurred (Fryer & Nakao, 2009). So too, teacher attitude to chatbot use, as with many activities, has also been seen to impact upon the classroom success of these technologies (Bii, Too, & Mukwa, 2018), or lack thereof, and this would likely transfer over to any use of digital assistants. Increasingly then, factors considered essential for the design of foreign-language learning chatbots need to be taken into consideration when developing interactions with such systems, and this can be seen with the digital assistant Lily (Malewar, 2018). In this case, Lily attempts to incorporate app-based content alongside assistant use to provide an immersive language experience that includes interactive conversations, real-time translation, vocabulary games, and stories to go one-step beyond basic chatbots by incorporating artificial intelligence (AI) into the interaction process.

3

How can I use digital assistants?

While paramount for language learning, conversation practice can often prove difficult to obtain and if continually attending classes, expensive to engage in. Digital assistants can serve as a means of providing this practice, especially if integrated into the teaching and learning context both at home and in the classroom (Underwood, 2018). However, the long-term effect of digital assistants and students' perceptions of digital assistants as language learning companions, along with the usefulness of such devices for language learning, remains until now largely unexplored. What we do know is that they can provide a means of interaction that lowers the affective filter (Brown, 2014) of students, which can then lead to the promotion of speaking that is not necessarily contrived. Speaking to machines, and seeing or hearing appropriate responses actioned, provides learners with a reason to speak that is inherently motivating and meaningful (Underwood, 2018).

The main challenges presented in today's language learning classrooms, as Hsu (2105) points out, is the lack of time available to provide students with input and output opportunities from a stress-free environment. The opportunities that a digital assistant may then afford is the ability to free up class time, allow for more focused and personalized instruction, and provide learners with stress-free opportunities for increased input exposure and output practice in terms of both quality and quantity. Such interaction, particularly one that involves peer collaboration and learner-centered tasks in a classroom-based context, can help establish a safe-speaking environment for students (Dornyei, 2018). In the case of voice-interaction, particularly in RALL (robot assisted language learning), students have presented with lower levels of anxiety coupled with an "increased positive attitude toward learning", and "believed they were learning more effectively, which helped them boost their motivation" (Alemi, M., Meghdari, A., & Ghazisaedy, 2015, p. 523). Dizon (2017) also recognizes the voice user interface of digital assistants to be useful, particularly when combined with in-class teacher-facilitated interactive practices that rely on the use of "personalized, computer-mediated instruction as an approach to extend the reach of the classroom" (Moussalli & Cardoso, 2016, p. 325).

The significance, then, that this kind of technology affords teachers if integrated into the classroom is that it can be used to provide support for tasks and classroom management while also delivering opportunities for voice-driven learning for students. Also, for learners, both in and outside of the classroom, these devices have the potential to provide one-on-one individualized support for engaging in language learning and language practice (Winkler & Sollner, 2018), as well as for learning in general.

4
What types of digital assistant exist?

There are several types of digital assistant, and the most well-known may be Alexa, Bixby, Cortana, Google Assistant, and Siri. All of these are capable of a variety of tasks including voice interaction, music and video playback, creating to-do lists, setting alarms, streaming media, playing audiobooks, telling stories, playing trivia games, and providing real-time information (such as news, weather, traffic conditions, and sports scores), while also controlling a variety of smart devices. Pressing a button, or using a wake-word, activates each assistant.

Alexa was developed by Amazon and initially released in November of 2014, and it can be found in devices such as the Amazon range of smart speakers. The wake-word can be set by the user, with the default being *Alexa*. The assistant is also available as an application for smartphones and tablets.

Bixby was developed by Samsung Electronics and initially released in April of 2017, and it is the voice-powered assistant used on the range of Samsung smartphones and tablets. It is activated with a button press.

Cortana was developed by Microsoft and initially release in April of 2014, and it is the virtual assistant for Windows 10 and other related Microsoft products (including smartphones, tablets, Xbox, band fitness tracker, surface headphones, and Windows mixed reality). It also runs on the invoke smart speaker, Android, and iOS. If the always-listening mode has been selected in Windows 10, then the wake-phrase 'Hey, Cortana" can be used to activate the assistant.

Google Assistant was developed by Google and initially released in May of 2016, and it is primarily accessible on mobile and smart home devices as well as Google smartphones and Android devices including Wear OS. It is also available as a stand-alone application for iOS. The wake-phrases for the assistant include "Hey, Google", and "OK, Google".

Siri was developed by Apple Inc. and released in October of 2011, and it is the virtual assistant that became part of iOS, watchOS, MacOs, the HomePod, and the tvOS operating systems. As an application, it was initially released in February of 2010 for iOS, and it can also be accessed through the latest version of the MacOS and Apple CarPlay. The wake-phrase for this assistant is "Hey, Siri".

Although Coniam (2014) did find that the accuracy of chatbots for use as conversation practice machines did need improvement before they could be extensively utilized as a language partner, Enge (2018) has since shown that the accuracy of digital assistants is increasing year-on-year. So too, as Underwood (2017) highlights, voice interaction technology has advanced more in the last 30 months than in the previous 30 years, with Nordrum (2017) concluding that error rates for voice-recognition systems are now nearly on par with that of humans. In an extensive study, which asked

4,952 questions of each digital assistant, with a focus on their ability to answer general knowledge questions, Google came out in the lead. The study also points out that by-and-large erroneous responses from digital assistants occurred as a result of poorly structured or obscure inquiries. It was also found that users were able to identify incorrect responses and were not misled by erroneous answers. A summary of these results is displayed in Table 1.

Table 1.
Digital assistant general knowledge test

Digital Assistant	Answers Correct
Google Assistant (on smartphone)	3,639 (74.7)
Cortana	2,944 (59.5)
Google Assistant (Home)	2,868 (58)
Alexa	2,195 (44.3)
Siri	1,616 (32.7)

Note. Numbers in parentheses are percentages.

When selecting a digital assistant for use with learners or alongside instructional delivery, it is important to understand that the accuracy of the content being received from a digital assistant, when asking general questions, is going to be dependent upon the source of the data that the digital assistant can access. Google assistant has access to *Google*, while Alexa relies on the computational knowledge engine WolframAlpha. Of note also, the Google Assistant has many abilities built-in, with users just needing to begin interactions. On the other hand, Alexa may need to have specific skills added to the device manually (like applications), but this can be completed either through the Amazon website or via voice command. Many of these skills are third-party and each will vary in terms of quality and what can be accomplished while using them.

Taking the above into account, the unique features of employing digital assistants with students for teaching and learning in the classroom include:

- The provision of voice-driven learning from a safe speaking space;
- dialogue-driven interactions requiring multiple as well as singular turn-takings;
- practice opportunities to develop fluency, as well as active (speaking) and passive (listening) skills;
- access to a variety of actions or skills to engage learning (game-based, story-based, drill-based, content-specific action-based interactions);
- one-on-one individualized language learning and language practice support; and,
- instant access to content that is authentic and factual, with such information coming from a known and trusted database.

5

What elements are behind the effective use of digital assistants in TESOL?

Working with digital assistants in the language learning classroom is mainly about creating more meaningful speaking opportunities that are integrated in sensible ways to prepare students to use that language in the future (Underwood, 2017). This is particularly important as our students will now be living with AI as part of their daily lives, and they need to know how to engage critically and actively with these intelligences. This is especially relevant now as 70% of children aged 8-17 are using voice-assisted technologies, predominantly for information searches, but also to ask questions, play music, and to get advice or help (UK Safer Internet Centre, 2018). This also illustrates that there is now no need to memorize facts or figures, as these are all available instantly. However, students do need to know how to assess this information and determine how best to apply it for their needs, for solving problems, for completing specific tasks, or for achieving particular outcomes.

Teachers incorporating digital assistants into the classroom or for use with learners need to think about what it is that the AI should be doing, and how this changes the role of language facilitation. For example, establishing an environment where students can work in an atmosphere that supports self, partner, and teacher collaboration with the AI, and one that seeks to provide a means of scaffolding and social interaction as they learn (Vygotsky, 1978). Utilization of AI can also assist teachers in identifying student knowledge gaps particularly when analyzing transcripts of interaction to identify learner needs (e.g., vocabulary improvement, and structure practice), while outside of the classroom, students can use them as language learning companions (e.g., helping them to complete homework, and providing access to additional tutoring or study programs).

Digital assistants for language learners can also provide students with the opportunity to go from the learning of speech to the written word, instead of the other way around. So, it changes the nature of learning. So too, instant access to translations, and with the ability of an AI to make phone calls and have conversations in any language on our behalf (for example, booking a haircut, see Alfa Tech, 2018) clearly illustrates that the reasons humans will have to learn a new language will change.

6

How do digital assistants lend themselves to TESOL?

Digital assistants offer several affordances, but also come with several shortcomings that you as a teacher will need to consider and aim to circumvent when implementing the technology.

Some of the main advantages that digital assistants present include:

1. Natural interaction, with instant real-time responses that can encourage motivation and learner engagement while lowering their affective filter.
2. Authentic content exposure, particularly when asking factual questions or for further information on a given topic, including spelling and vocabulary. This is effective for learning as it provides students with personalized, and as such, more useful feedback.
3. Active (speaking) and passive (listening) skills development, while also helping students focus upon pronunciation as they communicate their message or intents.
4. Interaction (Chapelle, 2015) that sees students being able to engage in the negotiation of meaning, obtain enhanced input, and direct their attention to linguistic forms.

5. Support for several learning methods and approaches (including game-play).

6. Additional learning pathways for students with various disabilities. This includes those who are visually-impaired, dyslexic, or have dysgraphia, along with those who may have hearing disabilities if screen-based digital assistants are employed.

Shortcomings might arise from:

1. Frustrations, when users commands and questions, or their responses are continuously misheard or not understood (especially if students have speech difficulties). This can be alleviated by the instructor guiding students with appropriate models that can be used, helping students understand why the miscommunication occurred, working with the assistant to have it understand what is trying to be communicated, and helping students to work out how to use language to get the answers that they need. This also allows teachers to focus on getting students to think critically, and to help them develop higher-order thinking skills.

2. Fossilization/stabilization might occur as the assistants can understand sentences and utterances that are not always grammatically correct. This does allow students to continuously engage with the device as they are understood and are able to communicate, and it also provides teachers with the opportunity to

provide better models for students to practice using with the device.

3. Privacy concerns might need to be considered as the device can record what is being said and asked of it. This does provide an opportunity to raise e-safety concerns and data protection questions with learners. Checking the transcripts of the device after class can also allow instructors to see how students interact with the assistant, and this provides opportunities to analyze student utterances for grammar issues and to see if new vocabulary is being integrated into their language output.

4. Accessibility: internet access needs to be stable and reliable for use with these devices. Otherwise, the device may not function at all or it may have trouble retrieving or playing back content.

5. Inappropriateness may arise with particular students asking questions that are rude or distracting. One way to counter this is to discuss responsibilities such as digital citizenship before using the digital assistants in class, that the device is going to know what they have asked it, and that others will also hear what they say.

6. Voice recognition may be an issue with a rowdy class or many students speaking at the same time. However, this could help develop turn-taking skills in students.

7
How can I start using digital assistants with students?

As with other technologies, the use of a digital assistant with language learners needs to be guided, with the teacher perhaps preparing content or worksheets that can be utilized with the digital assistant in order to promote the learning outcomes desired. It is a good idea to start small, and keep a list of voice commands or actions and skills handy for teacher and student reference, especially the ones that you would like to try, or find yourself and your pupils frequently using. Some examples are provided in the section *Photocopiable material*.

When starting out, it is also important to set guidelines of use for students. You may wish to allow only one student at a time to access the device. In this way, you can then begin to track the kinds of questions or phrases that students are using so that you can record the ones that work (or the ones you would like to provide modeling for). Use of the device in the classroom can also be added to the 'ask 3 before me' concept, where students need to talk to three peers in order to learn how to solve an issue or problem before going to the instructor.

Keep in mind that while *Google Assistant Actions* offers a variety of ways to interact with the Google Assistant,

Alexa Skills are developed both by Amazon and third-party developers so build quality and usability prior to use do need to be assessed. Assessing the potential use or modification of the Actions or Skills that are available through a digital assistant is always important, as it is with any learning material developed by another teacher for use with your own students and teaching style. This aspect is discussed in the section *How can I evaluate digital assistant use?*

Essentially there are three main ways that an instructor may wish to integrate the use of Digital assistants with learners: for classroom management and teaching aid purposes, for learning purposes, and as a personal language companion outside of the classroom for students themselves. This can be broken down into two broad categories: classroom management, and language-learning Actions and Skills. Both of these categories house content that leaners can access when using digital assistants as a personal language companion. The classroom management Actions and Skills sections looks at: teaching aids; timers and reminders; choosing volunteers; and team leaders; and streaming content. The language-learning Actions and Skills section covers: answering enquiries; vocabulary, pronunciation, and writing; listening and speaking; reading and writing; creating content; games; stories; songs and streaming content; formative assessment; and, additional voice user interface content. Although this provides a taste of what is available, the *Alexa Skills* section of the Amazon website provides a complete listing of all the Skills that are available. Each listing is available by category and provides information on how to utilize the Skill. On the other hand, *Google Assistant Actions* is the website that lists all of the Actions available for the Google Assistant. Each listing is available by category or search, and provides information about the skill as well as what devices and platforms it can be used on.

Classroom Management Actions and Skills
From a classroom management perspective, digital assistants provide a gamete of options to employ that include:

Teaching aids. Digital assistants can take on a number of the activities that a teacher's aide can do. It can be used by students individually to ask questions, and that can help to develop self-guided learning. It can also be used by teachers to answer any questions that students may pose during a teacher-directed activity or in things like homework checks (e.g., spelling words or providing answers to set questions). In this way, students can also hear models of speech to employ with the digital assistant, and see what kinds of answers return. If asking questions of students and they take a little too long to answer, you could request the digital assistant to provide a drum roll before the answer, and a round of applause if the answer is correct.

Timers and reminders. Timers can be employed to help learners to stay on track, to signify the end of an activity, and when it is time to transition to the next stage of an activity. Timers can also help with students who struggle with organization, serving as reminders to take medications for example. Timers are controlled by saying *'Start [five] minute time'*. Reminders can be set based on time or location, and are set by saying *'Set a reminder [for Brad to take his medication]'*, or *'Set a reminder for [students to change partners/take an exercise break]'*.

Choosing volunteers and team leaders. Random number generation can be used to select students based on their roll sheet order by saying *'Pick a number between [x] and [y]'*. Heads or tails (available by saying *'Heads or tails'*) or rock, paper, scissors (available by saying *'Play rock, paper, scissors'*) can also be used to select those who will be a team captain, those who might lead a presentation, take the first turn in an activity, and so on.

Streaming content. A variety of audio and video is available for streaming in the classroom through digital assistants. They are able to play white noise by saying *'Play [White noise/Rain forest sounds/Beach noises/etc]'*. Music can also be streamed by saying *'Play [artist name/genre of music/song name]'*, with video displayed on TVs and controlled from the device if using Chromecast or a Fire TV Stick by saying *'Play [artist name/genre of music/song name/movie name/TV episode name and number] on [Chromecast/Fire TV Stick]'*. Saying *'Play [podcast/podcast number]'* can also be used to playback podcasts for class listening, with other content like news also available by saying *'What's the latest news?'*

Streaming of audiobooks and the reading of a Kindle book is also possible using Alexa.

Language-Learning Actions and Skills

From a language-learning perspective, a number of options are available that both learners and teachers will find useful. Of note, when asking for information, the devices may also forward additional links to the device application on a smartphone, or these may appear on the devices display if it has one.

Answering inquiries. Specific fact-based questions can be asked of digital assistants, and these can be used to obtain general information or to help conduct specific tasks. For example: conducting research for a writing assignment; listening to information before performing a retelling task; completing questions assigned by the teacher on a specific topic; or for getting information on the vocabulary or themes under study in any given unit. Digital assistants can also be used to assist students in completing WebQuests, which are activities that require students to take on a role and perform certain tasks that involve both data collection and fact-checking guided by an inquiry-based process (Levin-Goldberg, 2014). Any factual-based question can be asked and answered on any topic or unit that students are studying, from hobbies through to travel and entertainment, along with statistical and historical information, recipes, conversions, jokes, and real-time information such as temperature, weather, store hours, and news. Unique Actions such as *Safari Mixer* which uses voice prompts to ask what kind of body parts an animal has in order to create a new animal, can see the Google Assistant asking questions of students. Once the questions are answered, an image of the animal that was created is then sent to the user's phone. The noise that new animal makes is played along with a fun 'fact' about the animal, leading to reading practice and vocabulary-development opportunities.

Vocabulary, pronunciation, and writing. A variety of simple questions can be used with digital assistants that can help with the acquisition of vocabulary, its pronunciation, and in the writing of these terms. These include:

- *'How do you spell [word/phrase]?'*
- *'What is the definition/meaning/synonym/antonym of [word/phrase]?' 'Define [word/phrase].' 'What is a [word/phrase]?'*
- *'How do you pronounce [word/spelled out word by letter]?'*
- *'What is the plural of [word]?'*
- *'Translate [word/phrase] to [language].' 'How do I/you say [word/phrase] in [language]?'*
- *'Repeat [word/phrase].'*

The teacher can also provide controlled practice tasks such as using the spelling ability of the assistant and having students ask it to spell hard-to-distinguish sounds (e.g. minimal pairs, such as *ship/sheep*). Just saying *'Tell me a new word'* to Google Assistant, or activating skills such as *Daily Word* on Alexa, can also be used to expand vocabulary.

Listening and speaking. Some skills such as *Ditty* (on Alexa) can help motivate controlled practice of specific structure. For example, students might say *'Ditty sing: If I were an animal, I'd be a cat.'* Games like Simon Says, can also be played using the assistant to actively practice listening skills. Student directed free talk can also be conducted, where students brainstorm their own questions (based on the unit theme), try asking them of the digital assistant in a kind of trial and error language use, and making note of and, depending on the level, discussing the answers that result. For lower levels, challenges such as, *'Which group can get all the answers from the digital assistant first?'* might inspire increased language output and input.

Reading and writing. As a reading assistant, Alexa has access to audio books and can read Kindle content. Google through *Story Speaker,* and Alexa through *Invocable*, allows for the development of actions and skills that can read back blocks of text that students have previously met during study, with the instructor developing questions for review and that move students on to more text and practice with content.

Creating content. Creating a voice-driven app cannot only help students in the reading and writing process, but it also gets students started with developing the kinds of digital skills that they will need in the future. During such a process, they will also need to think critically and creatively about language and communication in terms of how they use language, the questions that they need to ask, questions that they expect someone might ask a digital assistant, and all of the ways that those questions then need answering. A few templates exist that can be used to develop these skills without coding including free templates that are available from *Actions on Google, Alexa Blueprints,* and Google Voice Experiments such as *Story Speaker*.

Games. A variety of games exist that are worthwhile for language learning via a digital assistant. These include flash-card and trivia-based games that can be used for review, speaking, listening, vocabulary, or pronunciation practice. Both Google and Amazon have provided templates for the creation of these kinds of actions and skills, and this will be discussed in the section *How would I use a template to develop content for use with a digital assistant?* If a teacher is time poor, then they may rely on ready-made games that are available and include those that have a Jeopardy! style format or those that are similar to Twenty Questions. These might include *Mystery Animal*, where the assistant pretends to be an animal and users need to guess what animal it is by asking relevant questions. Questions need to be those that draw a yes or no answer, such as *'Do you have feathers?', 'Do you sleep at night?'*. It can be played on Google Home or on the website. An alternative for Alexa is *Twenty Questions*, where the digital assistant will attempt to guess the animal, vegetable, mineral, or music-related item that you or a student has chosen.

Stories. The educational value of storytelling and using stories for teaching is undisputed (Kalantari & Hashemian, 2015). The stories presented by digital assistants include short stories such as fairy tales as well as those stories that are quite interactive, and these are the choose-your-own adventure type stories. In either case, there are a number of ways to extend the potential that such stories provide. Students can listen to the stories, or work their way through them, and then complete a retelling task by paraphrasing the story in spoken or written form. They can also be asked to write a dialogs between two of the main characters (which in the choose-your-own adventure would include the student). They could also be provided with a handout from which they could be asked to summarize the story in three sentences, including the main character(s), the setting, conflict, climax, and resolution, or simply write one sentence on the theme of the story.

Teachers can also ask various follow-up questions and have students complete word-form charts for terms that they had to use in order to progress through interactive stories. For example, completing the participle, adjective, noun, verb, and adverb forms for their choices using a pre-fabricated handout. They can also compile a list of terms that they do not understand as they progress through the story, and later ask the digital assistant how to spell these words, the definition for them, a synonym, an antonym, and the translation. Students can also engage in writing their own choose-your-own adventure type stories using applications like

Story Speaker to create Actions for the Google Assistant or *Invocable* to create skills for Alexa. In these cases, they could be given a scenario such as being tech support where they need to think through a story process where various clients might telephone them with computer problems, and they need to offer solutions. They could also be given a scenario where they take a short holiday and have to choose between a cheap or expensive hotel, and go on to provide interactions and (mis)adventures that can be experienced while on holiday. An example is included in the section *How would I use a template to create content for use with a digital assistant?* If students are not up to the challenge of coding or using a template to create their own interactive stories, there are many types of templates available.

My African Safari is an interactive adventure for Alexa that takes users to Kruger National Park in South Africa, providing a variety of experiences over two chapters, eight stories, and 26 possible endings. An interactive story that spans various regions, such as a castle, garden, forest, and sea is that of *Magic Door*. The intent is to solve riddles, collect hidden items, and help magical creatures as the listener progresses through the story. The skill description states the following as the order to use in order to explore the entire land:

1. Take the garden path in the mountains to help the Princess find her crown.
2. Talk to the rabbit in the garden and find his eggs hidden beyond the gate.

3. Take the forest path in the mountains to help the gnome find the key to his home.
4. Take the boat across the sea to the tropical island to help a family of monkeys.
5. Follow the fiddle along the sea to a fortune teller who will direct you to a haunted lighthouse.
6. Travel up the bluff along the sea to gather items for the gnome with the flute.
7. Explore various lands to gather potion ingredients to grow a fern to the clouds.
8. Travel to the dark forest and search the witch's mansion for the wise wizard.
9. Journey past the garden gate to the holiday party in the princess' castle.
10. Search for the wizard in his tower, repair his broken mirror, and collect his wand.
11. Finally meet the wise wizard in the ancient temple and help him turn back time.

Songs, and streaming content. Songs are a staple of many language teachers' classrooms, and for good reason. They offer a variety of new vocabulary and can be chosen to suit the needs and interests of students, and they can be used to introduce slang and cultural aspects of a language. So too, the common repetitive pattern found in songs can also help learners practice syntax and semantics while they internalize language from a meaningful learning context (Romero, 2017). A number of sing-along Skills are available for Alexa, while Google Assistant can play back karaoke versions of songs. Further, Skills such as *Ditty* can be used by learners to turn any spoken phrase or simple message into a musical ditty by matching it to popular music (which can then be shared via Twitter). Example sentences from the text or what students create can be used for this purpose. If students are interested in creating music, then the Google Assistant *Mixlab* might be a more preferred Action, with users creating music by using voice-commands such as *'Play me a funky bass'* or *'Add some jazz drums'*. It can be played on Google Home or on the website. Also, for those students who might require white noise to concentrate, a variety of options are available by saying *'Play [white noise/rain forest sounds/beach noises/etc].'* Music can also be streamed by saying *'Play [artist name/genre of music/song name]'* with video displayed on TVs and controlled from the device if using Chromecast or a Fire TV Stick by saying *'Play [artist name/genre of music/song name/movie name/TV episode name and number] on [Chromecast/Fire TV Stick].'* Streaming potential for podcasts and other content is also available by saying *'Play [podcast/podcast number]'*; *'What's the latest news?'*; or *'Read'*, *'Get audible'*, *'Read Kindle'* if using Alexa to read aloud books.

Formative assessment. Opportunities exist for the teacher to access the transcripts of what students have said to the digital assistant, and to utilize the data to undertake continuous formative assessment. For example, if you have set an activity that requires students to use set phrases, vocabulary, and structures with the digital assistant you would be able to review the transcript of the session parsing through such websites as the *Compleat Lexical Tutor* in order profile the vocabulary and grammar used. This would then allow teachers to identify whicht students may need to work on further, and what could be covered more extensively in other classes and for review.

Additional voice user interface content. Teachers and students should keep in mind that digital assistants are not the only voice user interface that they have access to, and that there are a number of websites that also provide such opportunities. These include the following.

- *Dictation.io* is a website that uses Chrome to provide speech recognition for dictation. It helps to write emails, documents, and essays using only your voice.
- *Dumpling the Pug* provides a voice-user interface to control the actions of a virtual pug. Commands can be given in English or in Mandarin Chinese.
- *Forvo* is the largest pronunciation dictionary in the world. The aim of the website is to have a database consisting of all the vocabulary from every language in the world pronounced by native speakers. You can type in a word to hear its pronunciation.
- *The Peanut Gallery* is a website where users can select short movies to subtitle with text produced from their speech.

8
How can I evaluate digital assistant use?

The particular Actions or Skills that you might choose to employ with a digital assistant are numerous, and so you need to seek a means of how you might wish to evaluate the emergence of classroom success and the usefulness of digital assistant interaction. One of the easiest methods of doing this is to assess pre-existing and self-created actions/skills, particularly for use in the TESOL context, by using a prefabricated rubric (perhaps based on a Likert-type rating scale). Similar rubrics can also be applied by learners as they work with the device or after completing their assigned learning tasks. In these cases, such rubrics should be provided to students beforehand so that they can understand what will be assessed and expected of the device. This provides learners with an opportunity to ask any questions about the assessment procedure if they have them.

As most of the Actions/Skills that are available for use with digital assistants have not been designed for the TESOL classroom or the English language learner specifically, use of an evaluation rubric is perhaps essential to assess the quality of those that are freely available. It is also useful to apply such rubrics to any content that you may develop for yourself, as well as those developed by colleagues, to ensure that what has been created is a good fit for the teaching and learning context in which it will be deployed.

While it may be useful for busy teachers to apply pre-made rubrics, it may be better if the instructor formulates their own rubric so that it reflects the specific points, and the teaching environment, they wish to assess. A good source for this is Rubistar where there are a number of pre-made evaluation options as well as information on how to create unique context-sensitive evaluation instruments. The rubrics section of the *Resources list* also contains several other rubric-creation tools that may prove worthwhile to look over.

The following is a general, all-purpose rubric that can be adapted to specific teaching and learning environments in order to analyze and evaluate the applicability and usability of different technologies for digital language learning including digital assistants. A rating scale that goes from 1 to 5, with 1 being poor, 2 fair, 3 average, 4 good, and 5 excellent has been adopted in order to identify those aspects of technology integration that are weak, and those that align well with target objectives. The conceptual model used to develop the rubric is included in the *Photocopiable material* section, along with a blank template that you can utilize to create an individualized rubric for your own purposes.

Table 2.
Technology Integration Analysis and Evaluation Example Rubric

Aspect	Criteria	Score
The Technology (hardware or software)	Matches with core learning objectives (e.g., developing fluency, increasing listening practice, practicing vocabulary)	1 2 3 4 5
	Content assists with learner development (e.g., provides communicative fluency, grammar-based activities)	1 2 3 4 5
	Meshes well with the instructor (e.g., teaching style, classroom management techniques, time for development and incorporation into lesson plans)	1 2 3 4 5
	Appropriate for use with the target learner (e.g., age, language level, motivation)	1 2 3 4 5
Content	Content and software is error-free (e.g., no bugs; no spelling, grammar, or pronunciation errors)	1 2 3 4 5
	Provides relevant content and topics (e.g., authentic, timeless, up-to-date, holistically useful)	1 2 3 4 5
	Content can be modified, tailored, or guided for effective use (e.g., add content on demand, rework content to a lesson)	1 2 3 4 5
	Content is reusable (e.g., with the same students, across classes, across the curriculum)	1 2 3 4 5

	Content is shareable (e.g., not locked to a single student/class, distributable to other stakeholders)	1 2 3 4 5
Evaluation	Instructor use of the technology provides growth (e.g., leads to action research, pedagogical improvement)	1 2 3 4 5
	Easy to teach others how to apply the technology (e.g., develop a walkthrough)	1 2 3 4 5
	Variable assessment types (e.g., poll or multiple-choice for either formative or summative use)	1 2 3 4 5
	Reviewability (e.g., if assessable: grades can be seen, reviewed, and/or resubmitted by students)	1 2 3 4 5
Usability	Provides a learning shift (e.g., creates multi-modal learning, meets set standards; provides completion of competency pathways)	1 2 3 4 5
	Improves on past learning experiences (e.g., easier distribution or revision of content)	1 2 3 4 5
	Usefulness (e.g., provides formative/summative assessment; can be utilized for revision, homework, skills targeting)	1 2 3 4 5
	Distinctive, provides something old in a new way (e.g., polls students instantly with anonymity)	1 2 3 4 5

	Suitable for	in-class work	1 2 3 4 5
		out-of-class work	1 2 3 4 5
		individual work	1 2 3 4 5
		pair work	1 2 3 4 5
		group work	1 2 3 4 5
		with accompanying handouts	1 2 3 4 5
		alongside other technologies (phone/website/etc)	1 2 3 4 5
Resources		Community of content (e.g., a range of resources exist that can be adapted or used as-is)	1 2 3 4 5
Score		Total	____ /125

Ratings: 1 Poor 2 Fair 3 Average 4 Good 5 Excellent

9

What templates are available for digital assistant content creation?

Digital assistant content can be created by coding, but there is an increasing number of templates available for content creation of simple Actions or Skills, including the development of flash cards, trivia games, and choose-your-own-adventure type stories. All of these can contain multimedia elements alongside voice components. For the Google Assistant, these are available from the *Actions on Google* website, and for Alexa, from the *Alexa Blueprints* website. Google also offers several voice experiments, of which *Story Speaker* is one.

> *Alexa Blueprints* allows you to create personal Alexa Skills, using a variety of templates, to develop flash cards, trivia-based games, and stories through to customizations that can help extend the functionality of Alexa across devices such as the Echo smart speaker. Guided completion of templates is conducted while working online through the web page.
> *Actions on Google* allows you to create personal Google Assistant Actions using a variety of templates from flash cards and trivia-based games along with other actions to extend the functionality of the Google Assistant across devices such as the Google

Home smart speaker. Templates rely on configuration and content provided in Google Sheets. *Story Speaker* is one of the many existing Google Assistant voice experiments. It is a Chrome extension that allows you to use a Google Document to write a choose-your-own adventure type story that plays as an interactive talking story.

Development of content with each of these will be explored in more detail throughout the section *How would I use a template to create content?*

10
How do I select content for use or integration with a Digital Assistant?

One means of determining if the content you are looking at integrating into the classroom via a digital assistant is worthwhile is to use a framework like the substitution augmentation modification redefinition (SAMR) model (Puentedura, 2006; Hamilton, Rosenberg, & Akcaoglu, 2016). Such a model would allow you to assess the viability of the potential for the Action/Skill to enhance or transform the learning environment. The model consists of four segments with substitution and augmentation considered to be the enhancement sections of the model, while modification and redefinition are considered to be transformational (see Table 3).

Substitution is the utilization of technology in a way that simply replaces or directly substitutes a non-technological implementation. Here, you have to ask yourself what the gains may be for replacing the traditional teaching tool or technique with a technological one. For example, digital assistants could be used to spell out a word and provide its definition, synonym, antonym, and translation.

Augmentation also sees technology directly substitute traditional tools or techniques with technological substitutes, but a significant enhancement in use of the technology should result. Here, you would consider if using the technology being considered will augment or increase learning potential or student productivity in any way. For example, digital assistants provide all the facts that once needed to be learned, and they could be used when students create posters in order to conduct research that provides real-time information. They also provide real audio (animal noises), games (e.g., 20-questions, Jeopardy!), and quizzes, all of which result from the use of voice-driven interactions and turn-takings that can help students practice both their active (speaking) and passive (listening) skills.

Table 3.
The SAMR model

Enhancement	**SUBSTITUTION** Technology directly replaces an old way of teaching (direct substitute, no functional change)	**S**
Enhancement	**AUGMENTATION** Technology provides improvement (direct substitute, with functional change for the better)	**A**
Transformational	**MODIFICATION** Technology allows for significant task redesign (presents learning in a new way)	**M**
Transformational	**REDEFINITION** Technology allows for the creation of new tasks (implements something previously inconceivable)	**R**

Modification instead of replacement or enhancement, this section of the model looks at the design of a lesson or task and how technology use may provide increased learning outcomes. Here you would need to ask yourself if this use significantly alters the task for the better. For example, students can engage with a digital assistant for just-in-time learning where they use it to complete or check homework answers or to review content in a way that also provides additional language practice (speaking and listening) to assist with the development of fluency.

Redefinition, the final segment of the model, looks at using technology to promote a learning paradigm that is not possible to achieve without the incorporation of technology into the teaching and learning space. Here you would need to consider how the technology has helped the instructor or learner engage with content in a manner that would be previously inconceivable. For example, if students can use a digital assistant to check their pronunciation, develop their fluency, rely on it to provide them with one-on-one individualized support for engaging in language learning and language practice, and provide a device where they can also interact not just with an AI but with other learners as well (via voice chat).

Ultimately, the goal is to introduce digital assistants to learners in a way that allows their use to redefine the learning space for students, and you as a teacher, by replacing traditional teaching methods or learner interactions with alternates that add value. Keeping a model such as the above in mind when reviewing different actions/skills for use with the digital assistant and students will help you to understand how those actions/skills can capitalize on providing learning within your specific educational context, and if they are in fact worthwhile implementing.

11
How would I use a template to create content for use with a digital assistant?

The following guides cover the development of flash card based activities, trivia games, and choose-your-own adventure stories, and will work with *Actions on Google*, *Alexa Blueprints*, and Google Chrome. The choices of digital assistants, and the templates to follow are yours. However, please keep in mind that tools and websites do at times change the features that they offer and also the layout of the interface. Some may even become defunct. With this in mind, the following guides have been written in a way that any such changes will not impact on understanding the essential mechanisms behind the use of a template to create an Action/Skill.

11A. Actions on Google
Actions on Google allows you to create personal Google Assistant Actions using a variety of templates from flash cards and trivia-based games along with other Actions to extend the functionality of the Google Assistant across devices such as the Google Home smart speaker. Templates rely on configuration and content that is provided in Google Sheets, an example of which is in the section *Photocopiable material*.

a). Flash Cards

Step One – Preparation

To use Actions on Google, you will need to have a Gmail account. To begin to prepare your flash cards, you will also need to have a series for questions with hints, and a set of answers with some follow up information.

Step Two – Building the Action

1. Go to the Actions Console and log in with your Google account
2. Click on 'Add/Import Project' to create a new project. The 'Add Project' window will appear.
3. Select which language you want your action to support. (Additional languages can be added later.)
4. Type a name for the project, and then click on 'Create Project'.
5. Under 'More Options' select 'Templates'.
6. Click on the 'Flash Cards' option. You will then be taken to an overview page where you can enter information about the Action.
7. Click 'Build → Actions' and then 'Add Your First Action'.
8. In the 'Create Action' window, you should see the 'Flash Cards' option appear, then click 'Build'.
9. In the 'Personality' section, select one of the available options and then click 'Next'.
10. In the content section, click on 'Bulk Upload the Content for Your Action Using Google Sheets'.

11. Click on 'Make a Copy of the Pre-Filled Google Sheet for Editing' link and click 'Make a Copy'.
12. Update the 'Question and Answers' tab of the Google sheet with the name of your action. [see the section *Configuring the Google Sheet, Questions and answers tab*].
13. Update the 'Configuration' tab of the sheet [see the section *Configuring the Google Sheet, Configuration parameters tab*]
14. Once your Google Sheet is complete, return to the Actions Console and click 'Next' to move on to the 'Connect Sheet' step.
15. Copy and paste the Google Sheet's URL into the 'Add Your Sheet's URL to Upload Your Content' field, and then click 'Upload'.
16. Click on 'Create App'. The 'Overview; page will appear, showing you a notification that says 'Created'.
17. You are now ready to 'Test Your Action'.

Step Three – Configuring the Google Sheet

Open the Google Sheet downloaded during the Action creation process.

Questions and answers tab.

In this section of the Google Sheet, you will need to provide your questions under the heading 'Question'. An appropriate answer for each question needs to be placed under the heading 'Answer'. A hint for each question should then be included under the 'Hint' heading, and any follow up information in the final column under the 'Follow Up' heading.

Configuration parameters tab.
In this section of the Google Sheet, you can provide customization of the quiz title (QuestionTitle/AnswerTitle), which describes the subject of your questions and answers. You can also further customize the game by including additional parameters, and by providing the URLS to custom sounds. (For more details refer to the configuration parameters for the Google Sheet used with the Actions on the Google flash card game card template in the section *Photocopiable material*).

Step Four – Testing your action
1. In the 'Actions Console', click on 'Simulator'.
2. To invoke the Action, you can type or say 'Talk to my [name of app]. You can also test the Action through your phone or Google Home if the device and the Actions project are using the same Google account.
3. Interact with your Action!

b). Trivia Game
Step One – Preparation
To use Actions on Google, you will need to have a Gmail account. To begin to prepare your trivia game, you will also need to have a series for questions with a set of answers (one being correct and two distracters). You can also provide some follow-up information for each

question if desired, along with difficulty, and categorical information.

Step Two – Building the Action

1. Go to the Actions Console and log in with your Google account
2. Click on 'Add/Import Project' to create a new project. The 'Add Project' window will appear.
3. Select which language you want your action to support. (Additional languages can be added later.)
4. Type a name for the project, and then click on 'Create Project'.
5. Under 'More Options', select 'Templates'.
6. Click on the 'Trivia' option. You will then be taken to an overview page where you can enter information about the Action.
7. Click 'Build → Actions' and then 'Add Your First Action'.
8. In the 'Create Action' window, you should see the 'Trivia' option appear, then click 'Build'.
9. In the 'Personality' section, select one of the available options and then click 'Next'.
10. In the content section, click on 'Bulk Upload the Content for Your Action Using Google Sheets'.
11. Click on 'Make a Copy of the Pre-Filled Google Sheet for Editing' link and click 'Make a Copy'.
12. Update the 'Question and Answers' tab of the Google sheet with the name of your action. [see the section *Configuring the Google Sheet, Questions and answers tab*].

13. Update the 'Configuration' tab of the sheet. [See the section *Configuring the Google Sheet, Configuration parameters tab*]

14. Once your Google Sheet is complete, return to the Actions Console and click 'Next' to move on to the 'Connect Sheet' step.

15. Copy and paste the Google Sheet's URL into the 'Add Your Sheet's URL to Upload Your Content' field, and then click 'Upload'.

16. Click on 'Create App'. The 'Overview' page will appear, showing you a notification that says 'Created'.

17. You are now ready to 'Test Your Action'.

Step Three – Configuring the Google Sheet

Open the Google Sheet downloaded during the Action creation process.

Questions and answers tab.

In this section of the Google Sheet, you will need to provide your questions under the heading 'Question'. An appropriate answer for each question then needs to be placed under the headings 'Correct Answer', 'Incorrect Answer 1', and 'Incorrect Answer 2'. Any follow up information that you would like to include can be placed in the final column under the 'Follow-Up' heading. This could be something like additional facts concerning the correct answers. You can also add a column 'Difficulty/Grade Level' and enter the values 'Easy', 'Medium', or 'Hard' for each question. A 'Category/Topic' column can also be added as well, which might include 'Movies' or 'General Knowledge' for example.

Configuration parameters tab.
In this section of the Google Sheet, you can provide customization of difficulty and/or category of questions, include other parameters, and provide the URLS to custom sounds. (For more details refer to the configuration parameters for the Google Sheet used with the Actions on Google trivia game card template in the section Photocopiable material).

Step Four – Testing your action
1. In the 'Actions Console' click on 'Simulator'.
2. To invoke the Action, you can type or say 'Talk to my [name of app].' You can also test the Action through your phone or Google Home if the device and the Actions project are using the same Google account.
3. Interact with your Action!

11B. Alexa Blueprints

Alexa Blueprints allows you to create personal Alexa Skills, using a variety of templates to develop flash card and trivia-based games, listening and story-based quizzes, simple theme-based stories, and many other Skills. These include customizations that can help extend the functionality of Alexa across devices such as the Echo smart speaker. Guided completion of templates is conducted while working online through the web page.

a). Listening Quiz Blueprint

Example

You: *Alexa, open Aviation Prep.*

Alexa: *Let's practice for your upcoming aeronautical knowledge test on meteorology. Listen carefully, then answer the question to test your knowledge. Let's begin. To describe the amount of cloud cover in an area forecast the term 'okta' is used. One okta means one eighth of the sky is covered by cloud, four oktas means that half of the sky is covered by cloud, while 8 oktas means complete cloud coverage (i.e., overcast). In area reports and low-level area forecasts, however, rather than referring to oktas, the amount of cloud cover will be indicated by abbreviations: SKC (sky clear), 0 oktas; FEW (few clouds) 1 to 2 oktas; SCT (scattered clouds) 3 to 4 oktas, BKN (broken clouds), 5 to 7 oktas; and OVC (overcast), 8 oktas. Now, how many oktas does the abbreviation SCT refer to?*

You: *Er... three to four.*

Alexa: *Great work. Let's continue.*

Step One – Overview

This listening quiz will present some information along with a question that you will need to answer. The blueprint is ideal for practicing listening and recalling information, and it can be customized for different levels or topics.

Step Two – Creation

1. Write a passage and break it down into sections.
2. Write custom questions and answers for each section.
3. Name the skill.

Step Three – Usage

1. Follow Alexa's instructions and listen carefully to the content.
2. Pay close attention and answer questions as best as you can.
3. Replay as often as you like in order to get full points.

b). Story Quiz Blueprint

Example

You: *Alexa, open Spooky Story.*

Alexa: *You are spending the weekend at the Paradise Hotel, which was a booming business during the eighties. Local residents now avoid it, saying that it is haunted by a ghost named Rasper. Let's look around. You enter the hotel and walk up to the third floor, where you're staying in room 306. [...] You hear a voice: 'A stranger! I'm Rasper. Help me rest*

in peace by answering my questions. What is the number of the room you are staying in?'
You: *Uhh... room 306.*
Alexa: *Good memory. It is room 306.*

Step One – Aim

Create a story and test your memory. You can be very creative with story details, and create some tricky questions. For example, using numbers like *'How many birds did you hear tweet by the lake?'*; using descriptions like *'What color was the sign on the door?'*; using locations like *'Where was the coat hanging?'*; and using types of things like *'What kind of plants grow in the garden?'*

Step Two – Creation

1. Write a story with an introduction, multiple plot sections, and an ending.
2. Write custom questions and answers for each plot section.
3. Customize the narrator's prompts.
4. Name the skill.

Step Three – Usage

1. Open the skill.
2. Follow Alexa's instructions and listen to the story.
3. Pay close attention and answer the questions correctly.
4. Answer as many questions correctly as you can in order to beat the game.

c). Fairy Tale Blueprint

Example
You: *Alexa, open My Fantastic Fairy Tale.*
Alexa: *Welcome to My Fantastic Fairy Tale. This story has two blanks in it. To change a blank, say 'Alexa, undo.' Let's get started. Please say a name for the Princess.*
You: *Hyonhee.*
Alexa: *You said Hyonhee. Great. Are you ready to start listening to the story?*

Step One – Aim
Create an interactive prince and princess-themed tale.

Step Two – Creation
1. Get inspired by the sample story.
2. Customize it, or start from scratch.
3. Drop in sound effects, fun expressions, and pauses.
4. Create interactive 'blanks' to fill in while you listen.
5. Choose a name for the skill.

Step Three – Usage
Gather an audience. When you play the story, Alexa asks listeners to fill in the blanks and then reads the story to them.

11C. Choose-Your-Own-Adventure Story

Story Speaker is one of the many existing Google Assistant voice experiments. It is a Chrome extension that allows you to use a Google Document to write a choose-your-own adventure story that plays as an interactive talking story. It can also be modified and used to read blocks of text that students have previously met during study, with the instructor developing questions for review and that move students on to more text and practice with content.

Preparation

You will need to have already prepared a choose-your-own-adventure story, or have permission to use one that someone else has developed that you want to convert to an Action. The stories do not have to be very long but they need to have a decision tree that drives the forks provided as selections to the user. A mind-map program could be used to create the decision tree.

Begin by sketching out your story and writing it in blocks, with each block having a series of questions (forks) that will take the reader/listener to another story block. Story block questions might include:

1. People/creatures/things that the hero has met (friends, travelling companions, mythical creatures, peripheral characters).
2. Inventory that the hero carries/loses/requires (artifacts, clothing, food, money, weapons).

3. Possessing special abilities or knowledge (actions undertaken, meeting location objectives).
4. Achieving a goal (reaching a destination, slaying an enemy, finding love, finding a treasure, rescuing a prisoner or a princess).

Each story block then links to others, depending on the fork chosen by the reader/listener, until they each a story ending. Here are five possible story endings.

1. The protagonist dies.
2. The protagonist is captured.
3. The protagonist fails in the quest.
4. The protagonist finds love
5. The protagonist finds a treasure.

Once your story is complete, you will be able to use it to create an Action using the Google Voice Experiment Story Speaker.

Step One – Getting Started
To use *Story Speaker*, you need to install the Chrome extension.

1. Download and install the Chrome browser, then open it (if not already installed on your device).
2. Add the Story Speaker extension to the Chrome browser.
3. Open a new Google Document.
4. Click on the 'Add-ons' menu item, and select 'Story Speaker'.

5. Choose either the 'Basic Template' or the 'Advanced Template'. This guide will use the 'Basic Template'.
6. Click 'Yes' to clear the document and have Story Speaker load the Basic Template.

Using the basic template

1. From within the template, there are some links to a video, and Story Speaker Docs'. It is advisable to both watch the video and read the document before moving on.
2. You can then begin to cut and paste your previously created choose-your-own adventure story into the Google Document.
3. Normal text represents Text-to-Speech (TTS), and this will be read aloud by the Google Assistant. Text that is in bold defines how the story will work, for example: it might represent choices that the listener can select to go to another story block. Story blocks need to have the same level of choice, and need to be indented to the same level across the page.
4. Each story should have a title and an intro, but an author is not required.
5. Paths are the smallest section of a story. They have a bold line for a choice that a user can make (e.g., **If you say "right"**), and an unbold line for what the user will then hear (e.g., You walk down the path to the right).
6. Forks are moments when the listener can make a choice. To create a fork, indent a path below

another path. For example, **Intro** is used to provide an introduction that presents a choice. The path then needs to be indented one level and the choices provided.

7. Choices can be provided with **If you say " "**.

8. Otherwises can be used to respond to listeners when they do not choose one of the choices provided. They are created in the same way as a path with a bold line (e.g., **Otherwise**) and an unbold line for what the user will then hear (e.g., Sorry, I didn't catch that. Try saying 'right' or 'left'.

9. Story endings should use [[END]]. When the listener reaches an end, they will be given a choice to go back and restart the story. There can be multiple endings.

10. There are a number of other features and an advanced template to explore. However, the above should get you started, especially when reviewing the Story Speaker Choose-Your-Own Adventure Example included in the section *Photocopiable Material*.

11. When you are ready to see how your story plays, select 'Play Your Story" from the sidebar on the right of the Google Document.

You can choose to play the story in a chat preview box or on your Google Home device.

12

What are the key points behind digital assistant use in the TESOL context?

Working with digital assistants for the teaching and learning of languages sees several key points emerge when considering their use with students inside and outside of the classroom:

- AI use, through digital assistants, provides voice-driven learning from a safe speaking space, with stress-free speaking opportunities allowing for increased input exposure and output practice that can lead to increased student motivation.
- Teacher attitudes towards activities, or the use of a particular technology, can influence how students perceive and engage with it, which, in turn, either inhibits or enhances the effect that technology can have on learning.
- Purpose of use is important, and instructors should encourage the use of a variety of activities with the devices, selecting those that help develop fluency as well as active (speaking) and passive (listening) skills (e.g., vocabulary checks, translation, and story-based, drill-based, game-based, or content-specific action-based interactions).
- Aim to utilize the technology to add value to the learning process, and to redefine the learning space for students, (e.g., as a classroom aid, and

by providing the means for students to use it as a personal learning companion).

- Access to authentic content through one-on-one interaction with these devices provides personalized learning and feedback opportunities to learners. It also provides instant access to content that is authentic and factual, with such information coming from a known and trusted database. (Note: always ensure that safe-search is turned on.)
- Students need to be guided with appropriate language models to use when speaking to the AI within these devices, and instructors will need to help students work out how to use language to get the answers that they need. In other words, help students to engage with the device by thinking critically about what they can ask, and how what they ask can be reworded if the device does not provide an appropriate response, thereby promoting the development of higher-order thinking skills.
- It is important to establish guidelines for device use, and what is appropriate to say and not to say (e.g., cover aspects of digital citizenship with students). Policies of use might also include unplugging the device when not in use, and having students understand the privacy issues involved with using such devices.
- Voice-recognition may be lower in a rowdy classroom but this can be used to develop student turn-taking skills, while also helping

learners to be more considerate and to begin listening more to each other when they need to communicate with the device.

- Provide support through the device for several learning methods/approaches, including game-play and interaction that help students engage in the negotiation of meaning, sees them obtain enhanced input, and directs their attention to linguistic forms.
- Check transcripts produced by the device to analyze and evaluate student use of structure and vocabulary, to see how they communicate with the AI, and what might need to be focused upon in later lessons or in review.
- Employ an evaluation rubric to assess the quality of the actions/skills available in order to determine their appropriateness and viability for enhancing language learning.
- Ensure that there is a reliable and stable internet connection available for the device to use. Otherwise, it may not function at all or it may have trouble receiving or playing back content.

Although not new, it is only now that voice-driven interaction with machines is beginning to change the way we use language and, to some extent, the nature of learning itself. Rather than communicating solely human-to-human, we are increasingly communicating human-to-machine, and machine-to-human. The rise of this kind of communication also begins to raise questions about the need to embody additional languages within humans as well as robots, and in turn, why we might want or need to learn an additional language. For now, however, as with any technology, teachers should analyze and evaluate how and why voice-assisted language learning with AI, through the use of digital assistants, is worthwhile before integrating it within the teaching and learning context. It is also important to adapt any technology use to student and curriculum needs, remembering that it is not the technology that drives learning but the pedagogy put in place behind the technology that ultimately leads to learning outcomes. Yet, with access to instant real-time information (including translation, spelling, diction, and fact-based information), the opportunities that digital assistants and voice user interfaces afford language learners is well worth exploring.

13
Lesson plan guides, and example implementation

Provided here are lesson plan guides, focusing on the use of digital assistants in the language learning context, as well as examples for implementing various Actions/Skills in the educational context. The guides are meant to assist in the understanding of how to develop a detailed lesson plan, and to help describe what each component or stage of a lesson may cover. The example implementation is intended to provide a use-case scenario detailing the techniques required to apply effective use of a digital assistant in a real-world setting.

The content covered here includes:
- Lesson plan general guide
- Lesson plan guide for digital assistant use in the classroom
- Example implementation: digital assistants

Lesson Plan General Guide	
Teaching Context	
Level of Proficiency	Student language level (e.g., beginner, intermediate, advanced).
Level of Maturity	Student age range (e.g., young learners, adults).
Lesson Length	Time allotted for the class (e.g., 35-45 minutes).
Lesson Topic	Major theme or focus of the lesson (e.g. numbers and time).
Objectives	Lesson aims (e.g., to teach students how to tell the time and date accurately).
Outcomes	Learning outcomes (e.g., students will be able to read analog and digital timepieces).
Relevant Prior Learning	Anything that students need to know before starting work on this lesson's content. (e.g., students need to have completed Chapter Two of the book, and have previously met language associated with appointments, calendars, and timekeeping).

Teacher Preparation	
Hardware	Types of computer or peripherals required (e.g., USB sticks, MP3 players).
Software	Name of software used (e.g., Photo Story 3, Microsoft Word).
Webpage Links	Hyperlink to web resources (e.g., www.google.com).
Additional Resources	Other necessary materials for the lesson (e.g., handouts, worksheets, textbooks).

Procedure			
Stage and Timing	Objective	Teacher	Students
Review Stage (if required, 5 minutes)	Focus of stage (e.g,. encourage the use of previously acquired language).	Indicate what the teacher says and does in each stage of the lesson.	Provide expected examples of student behavior.

Warm-up Stage/Pre-Technology Use (10 minutes)	Focus of stage (e.g., introduce new concepts and language to students in a meaningful manner).	Indicate what the teacher says and does in each stage of the lesson.	Provide expected examples of student behavior.
Main Stage/ Technology-based Activity (20 minutes)	Focus of stage (e.g., allow students to utilize technology to become familiar with and apply the concepts and language content introduced in the lesson).	Indicate what the teacher says and does in each stage of the lesson.	Provide expected examples of student behavior.

Practice Stage (15 minutes)	Focus of stage (e.g., allow learners to utilize the skills and language that they are expected to acquire during the lesson in a practical way).	Indicate what the teacher says and does in each stage of the lesson.	Provide expected examples of student behavior.
Lesson Summation Stage/Post-Technology Activities (10 minutes)	Focus of stage (e.g., instructor reinforces the importance of language concepts and skills acquired, stating how they will be useful in forthcoming lessons).	Indicate what the teacher says and does in each stage of the lesson.	Provide expected examples of student behavior.

Further Considerations	
Follow-Up Activities	Prepare material that can be applied in a follow up class. Also, be ready with activities for students who complete their class work earlier than expected.
Contingency Plan(s)	Always prepare an alternate teaching scenario in case of any problems. For example, a sudden power outage, or a timetabling issue could make the assigned room unavailable.
Evaluation	Reflect on what worked well, and what did not, and how you might deliver the lesson differently or improve upon it when running it again.

Lesson Plan Guide for Digital Assistant Use in the Classroom	
Teaching Context	
Level of Proficiency	Beginner to advanced.
Level of Maturity	Adaptable for use with young learners through to adults.
Lesson Length	One lesson (at some point during the week or term). Time allotted for the activity: 50 minutes. Homework completion components (if required).
Lesson Topic	Wh-type question practice, and answer word order.
Objectives	1. Understand and use wh-type question words (e.g., What? Where? Who? When? Why? How?). 2. Generate authentic wh-type questions to use in a real-world context. 3. Understand the appropriate word order for answering wh-type questions.
Outcomes	1. Students will show evidence of the ability to use the structure of WH-type questions correctly. 2. Students will show evidence of the ability respond to WH-type questions using appropriate word order. 3. Students will speak with a digital assistant to get answers to the questions that they have developed.

Relevant Prior Learning	None, although students could have been introduced to the grammar and use of wh-type questions previously, in which case the lesson can serve as a solidification and review.

Teacher Preparation	
Hardware	A specific digital assistant Device (e.g., Amazon Echo, Google Home); or a computer, smartphone, tablet with a microphone and digital assistant running on the platform. Stable internet access.
Software	Digital assistant built-in Actions/Skills
Webpage Links	YouTube videos practicing wh-question type use.
Additional Resources	Handout for student reference, and to work on during class (and/or homework if desired).

Procedure – Day 1 of 1			
Stage and Timing	Objective	Teacher	Students
Review Stage (10 minutes)	Remind students of the type of wh-type questions that exist. Provide a word order with examples.	Teacher writes wh-type question words on the board (e.g., What?, When?, Who?, When?, Why?, How?), prompting students after each one is written (e.g., What time is it?).	Students answer the questions that the teacher prompts them to answer using appropriate word order. Responses can be whole-class, or individual. (Use the digital assistant to select a random corresponding to the roll sheet).

Warm-up Stage/Pre-Technology Use (15 minutes)	Introduce question words and the reason why each may be asked, and introduce example questions for each. Focus on the grammar, and how to answer each type.	Point out the specific word order required for answering wh-type questions. For example, asking about the subject of a sentence.	Students can practice with a partner, asking and answering various types of questions from the examples provided by the instructor. (Set a timer with the digital assistant in order to know when to transition to the next phase of the lesson).

Main Stage (15 minutes)	Practice writing and asking questions with an accompanying worksheet.	Ensure that students develop at least five questions, each using a different question word, and following appropriate word order.	Students ask the digital assistant to answer their five questions, writing down the answers that they hear.

Lesson Summation Stage/Post-Technology Activities (10 minutes)	Students should be reminded of the lessons' goals. They should be able to practice asking and answering with various question words, and be able to understand the appropriate word order to achieve this.	Remind students of what they should have achieved, and ask them to practice asking questions to the digital assistant and writing down the answers.	Students should have completed the associated worksheet (see the section *Photocopiable material*), writing down five questions to ask the digital assistant, and the answers that they heard. This could also be assigned for homework.

Further Considerations	
Follow-Up Activities	Students can ask their questions to partners to see if their partners' answers match those of the digital assistant. While pairs are waiting to speak to the digital assistant they can ask their partners the questions they created. This can help to develop listening-comprehension skills, as well as help students to critically reflect upon the answers that they receive.
Contingency Plan(s)	The entire lesson can be used with the Digital Assistant component swapped out for peers or the teachers (or for parents, siblings, or friends if being used in a homework scenario). Alternatively, the next lesson in the course syllabus could be ready for use in case there is a problem. Additionally, some short time-filler activities, like language games, can be prepared to fill in the time if technological problems occur. Several activity sheets, for review of previous material, could also be on hand to allow those students who complete the activities early to keep busy with language content.
Evaluation	What are the biggest frustrations for implementation? Can these be remedied next time? What are the successes of the lesson? What did students get out of this activity? Can more language practice be provided?

Example Implementation:
Digital Assistants

The Teaching and Learning Context

Speaking to machines, along with seeing or hearing appropriate responses actioned, provides learners with a reason to speak that is not contrived and one that is inherently motivating and meaningful. The significance, then, that this kind of technology affords teachers, if integrated into the teaching and learning context, is that it can be used to provide support for tasks and classroom management while also delivering opportunities for voice-driven learning for students. Also, for learners, both in and outside of the classroom, these devices have the potential to provide one-on-one individualized support for engaging in language learning and language practice, as well as for learning in general.

Teaching Material

The teaching material associated with Digital Assistant use can be broken down into three: the Actions/Skills, the hardware, and the implementation of pedagogy behind learning content.

The Actions/Skills

The Actions/Skills specific for use with this example with this lesson are built into the Google Assistant, but would require a Skill to be enabled for Alexa.

The hardware

The hardware is the device that houses the digital assistant. This may be a smartphone or it could be a smart speaker (such as Google Home, or Amazon Echo), or it could be a screen-based device such as the Google Home Hub or the Echo Show. No matter what device is being used, the account that is linked to it should ensure that parameters for privacy and safety are adjusted appropriately when using the device in the classroom (e.g., safe-search is turned on).

The learning content

Due to the flexibility behind the types of digital assistant available, and the types of Actions and Skills accessible through them, the learning content will vary on an activity-to-activity basis. It will, however, reflect the content that students are working on during class or for homework, as well as their personal interests. The key here is to implement this content in a way that leads to learning. Keep in mind that it is not the technology that drives learning but the pedagogy put in place behind the technology that ultimately leads to learning outcomes.

Procedure

As with a lot of technology use in the classroom, it may prove best to use one item per term or semester, so that students can become familiar with it and complete all their assignments or tasks when using it. This could prove especially the case with a digital assistant in the room, where students could use it to for various tasks including setting timers and reminders, selecting team leaders, using it in place of dictionaries and encyclopedias, and for engaging in pronunciation and speaking practice. To this end, a potential activity is introduced to illustrate an idea that can be applied to the use of digital Assistants in the TESOL setting. The idea presented here provides just one example, and is meant to illustrate how a digital assistant can be applied to learning. Ultimately, you will need to decide how best to integrate digital assistants within your teaching and learning context. The challenge will be to ensure that all students are able to make use of their voice in a way that empowers them, and provides them with meaningful interactions.

Example Implementation – Tongue Twisters!

Tongue twisters are often used to help students practice their pronunciation and improve upon their fluency. Google Assistant has access to tongue twisters built in but a *Tongue Twister* Skill will need to be enabled on Alexa.

Warm-up

Tongue-twister use is an easy way to provide a lesson warm-up that transitions students into speaking immediately. To begin practicing tongue twisters with students write, some of the more popular ones on the board, and ones that would help with your target learners' problem pronunciations. You could also ask students to write up, and speak out, some tongue twisters from their L1. Try them out for yourself in order to help create a connection with students.

Activity

The digital assistant can be used here to speak out a tongue twister for the class to engage with under guided practice. Students can also be provided with a tongue twister each, see the *Tongue Twisters!* sheet in the section *Photocopiable material*. They could then be asked to read through the list of tongue twisters together with the teacher or with their partner(s). The digital assistant can then be asked for a random number to select a student (perhaps using roll sheet order) who can then read out a tongue twister for everyone to complete for whole-class practice.

Practice

The activity can then be extended by placing students into groups, with the following written on the board or provided as a handout.

Get into teams of five.

Make your own tongue-twister.

Each person:

1. On a piece of paper, write your first name. (Pass the paper to the person on your right).
2. Write down something that he/she did. (Pass the paper to the person on your right).
3. Write down where he/she did it. (Pass the paper to the person on your right).
4. Write down when he/she did it. (Pass the paper to the person on your right).

5. Write down the reason why he/she did it. (Pass the paper to the person on your right).

This will give each group five tongue twisters.

Students might need to see some examples. Such as:

> *David drank a drink in downtown Denpasar at daylight to destress*
>
> *Noddy needed noodles in Neverland at noon to 'nom nom nom.'*

Tell students that they can ask questions to the Digital Assistant to help them create their tongue-twisters. These might include:

> *What are some actions that begin with the letter [...]?*
>
> *What are place names that begin with the letter [...]?*
>
> *What are emotions that begin with the letter [...]?*

Further practice

As either a test, or for those students who complete the writing of their individual tongue twisters early, the digital assistant can be used to repeat the tongue twisters that students are saying. It can also be used by them to see if they are pronouncing the sentences adequately. Additionally, they can ask the Digital Assistant to speak additional tongue twisters for them to practice.

14
Photocopiable material

This section of the book contains all the photocopiable handouts mentioned throughout the text. You can feel free to make as many copies as you require for teaching purposes and for use within your classes. Any other use or distribution should include a citation to the source of the content.

The content here focuses on providing invocations, and some example Actions/Skills that can be integrated into the classroom context for a variety of reasons. There are many more Actions/Skills available, either built-in or third-party developed. You can also work with various applications and templates to create content tailored specifically to your teaching and learning context, which the template examples, also included, will hopefully inspire you to do.

Every day, more and more digital language learning content is released, along with content that is transferable or that may transform teaching purposes. So, there is certainly a plethora of content available to us as teachers that has the potential for good use in the classroom. However, because of this, it is often difficult to assess the quality and usability of this content before we apply it, even if it is content that we ourselves have developed. As such, a conceptual model for thinking about how to assess the content that is available, or constructed by ourselves and other teachers, is included. A blank template from which to begin developing an evaluation rubric tailored to your specific teaching style and classroom context has also been provided.

Also provided is a lesson plan template that can be used for considering how best to integrate Digital Assistants within your classes. It is meant to act as a means to begin thinking about how to implement and evaluate aspects of what has been discovered through this book with your classes, and it should be supplemented with any necessary material. The staging as well as other aspects of the lesson should be adjusted as required.

The following photocopiable material is available:
- Digital assistant classroom and language learning use case examples
- Interactive stories – activity sheet
- Technology integration analysis and evaluation – rubric conceptual model
- Technology integration analysis and evaluation – rubric template
- Flash card example gsheet for use with the actions on Google flash card template – question and answer tab example
- Flash card example gsheet for use with the actions on Google flash card template – question and answer tab blank
- Flash card example gsheet for use with the actions on Google flash card template – configuration tab

- Configuration parameters for the Google sheet used with the Actions On Google flashcard template
- Trivia game example gsheet for use with the Actions On Google trivia template – question and answer tab example
- Trivia game example gsheet for use with the Actions On Google trivia template – question and answer tab example blank
- Trivia game example gsheet for use with the Actions On Google trivia template – configuration tab
- Configuration parameters for the Google sheet used with the Actions On Google trivia template
- A Story Speaker choose-your-own adventure example
- Lesson plan template
- Wh-Type question words example sheet (for use with the lesson plan guide)
- Tongue Twisters! (example implementation)

Digital Assistant Classroom
and Language Learning Use Case Examples*
*There are so many more available that can be found
by experimenting with what to ask!*

Classroom Management	Command
Timers	'Set a timer for [x] minutes/hours/days', 'Set [x] minute/hour/day timer'
Reminders	'Set a reminder [for Brad to take his medication]', 'Set a reminder for [students to change partners/take and exercise break/etc]'
Choosing volunteers	'Pick a number between [x] and [y]', 'Heads or tails', 'Play rock, paper, scissors'

Language Learning Vocabulary/Phrases	Command
Definitions	'Define [word/phrase'], 'What is a [word/phrase]?', 'What is the definition/meaning of [word/phrase]?'
Synonyms/Antonyms	'What is the synonym/antonym of [word/phrase]?'
Spelling	'How do you spell [word/phrase]?'
Grammar	'What is the plural of [x]', 'What is a [word or phrase form/grammar]?', 'What is the use of [word or phrase form/grammar] in English?'
Translation	'Translate [word/phrase] to [language]', 'How do I/you say [word/phrase] in [language]?'

Speaking

Pronunciation	*'How do you pronounce [word/spell out word by letter]?'*

Listening

Books	*'Read', 'Get audible [book name]', 'Read Kindle [book name]'*
News	*'What's the latest news?'*
Wikipedia	*'Wikipedia [topic]'*
White Noise	*'Play [white noise/rain forest sounds/beach noises/etc]'*
Streaming music	*'Play [artist name/genre of music/song name]'*
Streaming video	*'Play [artist name/genre of music/song name/movie name/TV episode name and number] on [Chromecast/Fire TV Stick]'*
Streaming podcasts	*'Play [podcast/podcast number]'*
Stories	*'Tell me [a story/a fairy tale]'*
Facts	*'Tell me [something interesting]'*

Fun	Assistant	Action/Skill
Interactive Stories	Alexa	*Magic Door, My African Safari*
	Google	*Magic Door, 'Let's read along with Disney'*
Music	Alexa	*Ditty, 'Sing a song'*
	Google	*Mixlab, 'Sing a song'*
Games	Alexa	*20-Questions, Simon Says, Spelling Bee, Spelling Master*
	Google	*Akinator , Freeze Dance, Mystery animal, Mystery Sounds, Simon says*
Jokes	Alexa/Google	*'Tell me a joke'*

Miscellaneous	Command
Weather	*What is the temperature?*
	What is the weather [today/for tomorrow/ in X]?
	When is the [next full moon]?
	When/what time is [sunrise/sunset]?
Astronomy	*How many planets are there?*
	What is the closest planet to the sun right now?
Animal/vehicle noises	*What noise does an [animal/vehicle] make?*
Math	*What is the [sum/product/difference/quotient] of [x] and [y]?*
Statistics	*What's the population of [place]?*
Capitals	*What is the capital of [state/country]?*
Celebrities	*Who is [famous person/celebrity name]?*
Inventors	*Who invented [item]?*
	Who was the inventor of the [item]?
Health/Anatomy	*How many [bones does the human body have]?*
	What does the [body part] do?
Hobbies	*What books did [author] write?*
	What is [book title/movie] about?
	What books would you recommend for [me/a x year old]?
	What is a good movie to see right now?
Cooking	*Find me a recipe for [food].*
	How do I make [food]?
	Convert [imperial] to [metric]

Finance	*How much is [x currency] in [y currency]?*
	What is the exchange rate from [x currency] to [y currency]?
Occupations	*What does a/an [x] do?*
	What is it like to be a/an [occupation]?
Shopping	*What time is [x] open until?*
	Where can I buy a/an [item]?

Development   **Tools**

Alexa   Alexa Blueprints

Invocable

Google Assistant   Actions on Google

Story Speaker

Actions/Skills   **Lists**

Alexa   Alexa Skills

Google Assistant   Google Assistant Actions

Digital Assistant: **Action/Skill:**

_____   _____

THEME	VOCABULARY
What was the theme of the story? (Write one sentence). _____ _____ _____ _____ _____ _____	*Words*
OVERVIEW	*Spellings*
Paraphrase the entire story. _____ _____ _____ _____ _____ _____ _____ _____ _____ _____ _____ _____ _____	

CONVERSATION	*Definitions*
Write a short dialog between two of the main characters.	

SUMMARY	Synonyms
Summarize the story in three sentences. Include the main character, the setting, the conflict, the climax, and the resolution.	
_____ _____ _____ _____ _____ _____	
_____ _____ _____ _____ _____ _____ _____ _____	**Antonyms**
_____ _____ _____ _____ _____ _____ _____ _____ _____ _____	**Translations**

WORD FORMS

Verb	Adverb	Participle	Adjective	Noun

Technology Integration Analysis and Evaluation – Rubric Conceptual Model			
Construct	Criteria	Item	Example
Site/App	Purpose	Is the app/site purpose clear?	Aligns with learning objectives presented in activities.
Site/App	Purpose	Is the content in line with the purpose?	Content provides learning (e.g., communicative-based).
Site/App	Teacher-fit	Is the app/site compatible with your teaching style?	Matches the style of the teacher implementing the content.
Site/App	Student-fit	Is the app/site appropriate for use with the target learners?	Matches the style of learners.
Content	Accuracy	Is the information correct?	No spelling or grammar errors.
Content	Currency	Is the information up to date or timeless?	Topics and information from the last 5 years.

		Can the technology (or the content that it offers) be tailored to learning?	Applicability (can add content on demand; can rework content to a lesson; can utilize it to complete objectives/projects).
	Adaptability	Can the content be reused?	Suitable across different classes and students in the teaching and learning context; can be designed or modified once and used across classes/students.
		Can content can be shared?	Means to distribute content to all students, between students, to other stakeholders (including Ss output), content locked to a single student/class.

Evaluation	*Professional development*	Can instructor use of the app/site be assessed?	Useful for action research, improving teaching skills.
		Am I able to teach others how to employ this effectively	Develop a walk-through.
	Assessment suitability	Can the app/site be used for formative/summative assessment?	Provides a range of assessment choices for learners/instructors (e.g. poll, multiple choice).
		Can grades be reviewed/resubmitted?	Allows students to redo work and resubmit before final grading.
Usability	*Significance*	How is the technology important?	Shifts learning (e.g., provides multi-modal learning; meets set standards; provides completion of competency pathways)

	Adds value	How is using the technology adding value?	Improves on past experience (e.g., Easier distribution or revision of content).
	Usefulness	How is the technology useful to apply?	Means of use (e.g., provides formative/summative assessment; can be utilized for revision, homework, or skills targeting).
	Uniqueness	How is the technology providing something special?	Provides something old in a new or unique manner (e.g., polls students with anonymity with instant results)
	Deployment	How is the technology best utilized?	Context of use (e.g., in- or out-of-class, individual- pair- or group-work; smartphone, website, printouts).

Resources	Existing content	Does teacher-developed content already exist?	Community of content (e.g., a range of resources exists that can be adapted or used as-is to meet current needs).
Format	Checklist	What scale or means will be used for rating the applicability/value of items?	Likert scale (e.g. questions can be scored from 1 to 5 to get a total percentage out of 100 for the technology).

Technology Integration Analysis and Evaluation – Rubric Template			
Construct	Criteria	Item	Example
Format			

Flash Card Example Gsheet for Use with the Actions On Google Flash Card Template – Question and Answer Tab Example

North American versus British English Vocabulary

Question	Answer	Hint	Follow Up
What is a couch in British English?	Sofa	This word begins with an S.	The word *sofa* comes from the Arabic word *Suffah* which refers to a wooden bench covered in blankets and cushions.
What is a flashlight in British English?	Torch	This word begins with a T.	Did you know that the idiom *carry a torch for someone*, means that you have unrequited love for that person.
What are bangs in British English?	Fringe	This word begins with an F.	Use of the word *bangs* for *fringe* comes from the stables. Horses' tails were sometimes allowed to grow to a certain length, and then were cut off in an even, horizontal trim called a bangtail.

Flash Card Example Gsheet for Use with the Actions On Google Flash Card Template – Question and Answer Tab Blank

Quiz Name				
Question	*Answer*	*Hint*	*Follow Up*	

Flash Card Example Gsheet for Use with the Actions On Google Flash Card Template – Configuration Tab	
Key	*Value*
Title	Dr. Kent's Traumatizing Test
QuestionsPerGame	3
QuestionTitle	American versus British English
AnswerTitle	British English
RandomizeQuestions	Yes
QuitPrompt	Traumatize you later!
AudioDing	(URL to audio file here)
AudioGameIntro	(URL to audio file here)
AudioCorrect	(URL to audio file here)
AudioIncorrect	(URL to audio file here)
AudioRoundEnd	(URL to audio file here)
AudioCalculating	(URL to audio file here)

Configuration Parameters for the Google Sheet used with the Actions on Google Flashcard Template		
Question Title	Describes the subject of your questions in prompts.	Short string
AnswerTi tle	Describes the subject of your answers in prompts.	Short string
AudioDi ng	The sound played after each question, prompting the player for a response.	Audio URL
AudioGa meIntro	Introductory music played when the game begins.	Audio URL
AudioGa meOutro	Music played at the end of the game.	Audio URL
AudioCo rrect	Music played after the player provides a correct answer.	Audio URL
AudioInc orrect	Music played after the player provides the wrong answer.	Audio URL
AudioRo undEnd	Music played when the round ends.	Audio URL
AudioCal culating	Music played while the game is calculating the score.	Audio URL
Randomi zeQuestio ns	No: questions are serially asked in the given category/difficulty or grade level. Useful for testing the grammar, pronunciation, and time length of questions. This only works when the total number of questions is less than 50, and should only be used for testing purposes.	Yes/no
GoogleA nalyticsTr ackingID	Record analytics associated with the Action via the Actions Console.	Adds the Google Analytics

		tracking ID
QuitProm pt	Customize the exit message used for when the Action ends.	Text-to-speech message
AutoAdd AnswerS ynonyms	BASIC: splits the answer provided in the data sheet and matches true with any of the split words. For example, *'Shortness of Brain'* could match as true when the answer is *'Shortness of Breath'*. Yes: collects synonyms for split-words, adds these to the answers array, then matches them to synonyms. No: matches with the exact answer string. If there are multiple answers for the same question then separate them using '|'. For example, 'before meals	before eating'.	BASIC/ Yes/ No

Trivia Game Example Gsheet for Use with the Actions On Google Trivia Template – Question and Answer Tab Example

The Traumatizing Trivia Test!

Question	Correct Answer	Incorrect Answer 1	Incorrect Answer 2	Follow Up	Difficulty/ grade level	Category/To pic
What is the fourth month of the year?	April	March	May	In the northern hemisphere, April falls in Spring.	Medium	Months
How many days are in November?	30	31	28	30 days has September, April, June, and November.	Hard	Months
What is the opposite of tall?	Short	Shorty	Shorter	The best things come in small packages!	Easy	Opposites
What is the plural of tooth?	Teeth	tooths	teeths	Most adults have 32 teeth in their mouth.	Easy	Plurals

Trivia Game Example Gsheet for Use with the Actions On Google Trivia Template – Question and Answer Tab Blank

Quiz Name:

Question	Correct Answer	Incorrect Answer 1	Incorrect Answer 2	Follow Up	Difficulty/ Grade level	Category/To pic

Trivia Game Example Gsheet for Use with the Actions On Google Trivia Template – Configuration Tab	
Key	Value
Title	The Traumatic Trivia Test!
QuitPrompt	Traumatize you later!
QuestionsPerGame	3
FirstChoice	Category/Topic
SecondChoice	Difficulty/Grade Level
DifficultyOrGradeLevelPrompt	Which difficulty would you like to begin with?
CategoryOrTopicPrompt	Which topic would you like now?
DefaultDifficultyOrGradeLevel	Easy
DefaultCategoryOrTopic	Months
DifficultyOrGradeLevelSuggestionChip1	Easy
DifficultyOrGradeLevelSuggestionChip2	Medium
DifficultyOrGradeLevelSuggestionChip3	Hard
CategoryOrTopicSuggestionChip1	Months
CategoryOrTopicSuggestionChip2	Opposites
CategoryOrTopicSuggestionChip3	(Additional category/topic here. E.g., plurals)

Configuration Parameters for the Google Sheet used with the Actions on Google Trivia Template		
AudioDing	Sound played after questions, prompting a user response.	Audio URL
AudioGameIntro	Introductory music for when the game begins.	Audio URL
AudioGameOutro	Music played when the game is over.	Audio URL
AudioCorrect	Music for when the player gives a correct answer.	Audio URL
AudioIncorrect	Music for when the player gives an incorrect answer.	Audio URL
AudioRoundEnd	Music for the end of a round.	Audio URL
AudioCalculating	Music for when the game calculates the player's score.	Audio URL
RandomizeQuestions	No: questions are serially asked in the given category/difficulty or grade level. Useful for testing the pronunciation, grammar, and time length of questions. This parameter only works when the total number of questions is less than 50, and should only be used for testing purposes.	Yes/No
GoogleAnalyticsTrackingID	To record analytics associated with the Action via the Actions Console.	Add Google Analytics tracking ID

QuitPrompt	Customize the exit message for use when the Action exits.	Text-to-speech message
DifficultyOr GradeLevelP rompt	Customize the prompt presented to the user regarding selection of difficulWhat ty.	A string, e.g., *Which difficulty level do you want to begin with?*
DefaultDiffic ultyOrGrade Level	Customize the default difficulty level.	A string, e.g., *Easy*
DifficultyOr GradeLevelS uggestionCh ip1	Customize the first selection chip displayed to the player for the game's difficulty level.	A string, e.g., *Easy*
DifficultyOr GradeLevelS uggestionCh ip2	Customize the second selection chip displayed to the user for the game's difficulty level.	A string, e.g., *Medium*

DifficultyOr GradeLevelS uggestionCh ip3	Customize the third selection chip displayed to the player for the game's difficulty level.	A string, e.g., *Hard*
CategoryOrT opicPrompt	Customize the prompt presented to the player regarding category selection.	A string, e.g., *Which topic do you want now?*
DefaultCate goryOrTopic	Customize the default category.	A string, e.g., *Vocabulary*
CategoryOrT opicSuggesti onChip1	Customize the first selection chip presented to the player regarding the game's categories.	A string, e.g., *Grammar*
CategoryOrT opicSuggesti onChip2	Customize the second selection chip presented to the player regarding the game's categories.	A string, e.g., *Pronunciati on*
CategoryOrT opicSuggesti onChip3	Customize the third selection chip presented to the player regarding the game's categories.	A string, e.g., *Opposites*

A Story Speaker Choose Your Own Adventure Example

Title: Tale of the Travelers
By: David Kent

START HERE

Intro
You and two friends have just arrived in Seoul. You want to stay in a hotel. You have two choices. The cheap hotel is only $50 per night. The expensive hotel is $150 per night. Which hotel do you choose?

> **If you say "expensive" or "the expensive one" or "the expensive hotel"**
> You and your friends are staying at the expensive hotel. The room is large and beautiful so you relax and unpack. Now you want to go swimming but your friends want to go shopping. What do you do?
>
> > **If you say "swimming" or "go swimming"**
> > You and your friends are swimming in the hotel pool. It is beautiful and so much fun! Now you are hungry and want to go eat, but your friends want to go shopping. What do you do?
> >
> > > **If you say "eat" or "go eat"**
> > > You go to a nice restaurant for dinner. The food is really delicious but now you really don't have a lot of money left. You want to go back to the hotel and write emails but your friends still want to go shopping. What do you do?

If you say "hotel" or "go back to the hotel" or "emails" or "write emails"

You go back to the hotel, write a few emails, and then relax for the rest of the day. In the morning you take the train back to Daejeon. You don't have a lot of money left but you had a lot of fun. You can't wait to go back to Seoul! [[END]]

If you say "shopping" or "go shopping"

You and your friends enjoy shopping but spend too much money. Now you can't pay for your hotel. You had to call home and get your parents to send you money. This is the end of your trip! [[END]]

Otherwise

Now that you're full, what will you do? Say "go back to the hotel", or "go shopping". The waiter is ready to kick you out of the restaurant.

If you say "shopping" or "go shopping"

You and your friends enjoy shopping but spend too much money. Now you can't pay for your hotel. You had to call home and get your parents to send you money. This is the end of your trip! [[END]]

Otherwise

The lifeguard is no longer on duty, so the pool is closed. Say "go eat" if you want to go to a restaurant, or say "shopping" if you want to go to a department store.

If you say "shopping" or "go shopping"?

You and your friends enjoy shopping but spend too much money. Now you can't pay for your hotel. You had to call home and get your parents to send you money. This is the end of your trip! [[END]]

Otherwise

It really is a lovely room, but it is starting to look like a nice day outside. Say "aquarium" or "department store." Get out and do something!

If you say "cheap" or "the cheap one" or "the cheap hotel"

You are staying in the cheap hotel. The room is very dirty so you don't want to stay in the room. You decide to go sightseeing. You can go to the aquarium or you can go shopping at Lotte Department Store.

If you say "aquarium" or "the aquarium"

The aquarium is great. There is a lot of fish, and you take a lot of pictures. But, now you're tired and hungry. You want to go back to the hotel to rest, but your friends want to get something to eat. What do you do?

> **If you say "hotel" or "go back to the hotel" or "rest" or "go to rest"**
>
> You go back to your hotel. Someone has broken into your room and stolen all of your belongings! Now you are stuck in Seoul with no way home. What a terrible trip! [[END]]
>
> **If you say "eat" or "go eat"**
>
> You and your friends get something to eat at a street vendor. You didn't have a lot of money to spend but the food was tasty. You go back to the hotel, and in the morning take the train back to Daejeon. You may not have had the best hotel, but you had a great time with your friends. You can't wait to go back to Seoul! [[END]]
>
> **Otherwise**
>
> The aquarium is a nice place to visit but you've spent too long here. Say "eat" or "hotel". Time to move on.

If you say "Lotte Department store" or "Lotte" or "department store" or the "department store"

You and your friends are shopping for souvenirs at Lotte Department Store. It's amazing! (And, they're expensive!) You are exhausted, and now you want to go back to the hotel, but your friends want to eat something. What do you do?

If you say "hotel" or "go back to the hotel"

You go back to the hotel and have a wonderful night's sleep. In the morning, you catch the train back to Daejeon. You give your souvenirs to your friends and tell them that Seoul is a very expensive place to visit. You think to yourself, "Next time I will stay with relatives!" [[END]]

If you say "eat" or "go eat"

You don't have much money so you decide to eat at a fast food restaurant. The food makes you feel sick and you have a stomachache for the rest of the trip! Your trip of a lifetime is over. [[END]]

Otherwise

The department store is closing, and you've spent all day shopping. Say "hotel" to go back to the hotel, or "eat" to curb your hunger.

Otherwise

Do you really want to stay in this dirty room? Say "aquarium" or "department store." It's really dirty here.

Otherwise

Do you really want to sleep on the streets? Say "expensive" or "cheap." Brrr, it's getting cold out here.

If you say "It's a mystery"

No, it's a choose-your-own adventure story!

Anytime you say "What is this?"

This is the story Tale of the Traveler by David Kent.

Fallback

Sorry, I didn't get that. Try asking once more.

Lesson Plan Template	
Teaching Context	
Level of Proficiency and Maturity	
Lesson Length	
Lesson Topic	
Objectives	
Outcomes	
Relevant Prior Learning	
Teacher Preparation	
Hardware	
Software	
Webpage Links	
Additional Resources	

Procedure			
Stage and Timing	Objective	Teacher	Students
Review Stage (if required)			
Warm-up Stage/Pre-Technology Use			
Main Stage/ Technology-Based Activity			
Practice Stage			
Lesson Summation Stage/Post-Technology Activities			

Further Considerations	
Follow-Up Activities	
Contingency Plan(s)	
Evaluation	

WH-Type Question Words Example Sheet

TO ASK

Question Words	Meaning	Examples
Who	Person	Who is he/she/that? He/she/that is MinSu.
Where	Place	Where do you live? In Seoul.
Why	Reason	Why do you go to bed early? Because I have to be at work early.
When	Time	When do you go to work? At 6am.
How	Manner	How do you go to work? I go by public transport.
What	Object Idea Action	What is it? It's a frog. What are you thinking about? I'm just day dreaming. What do you do? I am a teacher.
Which	Choice	Which one do you want? I want the cheap one.
Whose	Possession	Whose book is this? It's hers/his/theirs.
Whom	Object of the verb	Whom did you meet? I met the director.
What kind	Description	What kind of music do you like? I like all kinds of music.
What time	Time	What time did you get home? I got home at 9pm.

How many	Quantity (count)	How many students are there?
		There are five.
How much	Amount Price (non-count)	How much time do we have before class ends?
		Five minutes.
		How much is the fish?
		Five dollars.
How long	Length Duration	How long is a mile in kilometers?
		It's almost 1.61 kilometers.
		How long did you stay in Japan?
		I stayed overnight.
How often	Frequency	How often do you exercise?
		I exercise every day.
How far	Distance	How far away is your school?
		It's 5 minutes away by car.
How old	Age	How old are you?
		I'm 18.
How come	Reason	How come I didn't see you in class yesterday?
		I was sick

TO ANSWER

To ask about the subject of the sentence add the question word at the beginning. For example,

> *Sharon* writes great poetry.
> *Who* writes great poetry?

To ask about any other part of the sentence and there is an auxiliary (helping) verb, put the question word and the auxiliary verb in front of the subject. For example,

> She can speak *Korean.* – *What* can she speak?
> They are leaving *tomorrow.* – *When* are they leaving?

If there is no auxiliary verb and main verb is a form of be (am, is, are, was, were), put the question word and the form of *be* in front of the subject. For example,

> The movie was *interesting.* – *How* was the movie?

If there is no auxiliary verb and the main verb is not a form of *be*, put the question word and a form of *do* (do, does, did) in front of the subject. For example,

> They go to *the park* every Sunday.
> *Where* do they go every Sunday

> She wakes up **early**.
> *When* does she wake up?

> He ate **a hamburger**.
> **What** did he eat?

WORD ORDER

    a)   General: Question word + auxiliary + subject + verb
Where were you born?
I was born in _____.

    b)   Subject questions (with no auxiliary)
Who sang the song Gangnam style?
_____ sang the song Gangnam Style.
Which team won the 2018 World Cup?
_____ won the 2018 World Cup.

    c)   Object questions (with answers to the question the object)
Who is your favorite singer?
My favorite singer is _____.

PRACTICE

The kinds of questions to ask our digital assistant

- *What is the largest city in the world?*
- *What is the smallest country in the world?*
- *What is the tallest building in the world?*
- *Where is the Burj Kalifa?*
- *Which football team won the 2014 World Cup?*
- *How do you spell context?*

ASK ALEXA/GOOGLE ASSISTANT

1. Think of five questions to ask our digital assistant.
2. Write down the questions, and then the answers that you hear?
3. While waiting to speak to the digital assistant you can ask your partner your question.
4. Check to see if the answers they give are the same!

Who? _____
Assistant: _____
Partner: _____
_____
_____

What? _____
Assistant: _____
Partner: _____
_____
_____

Where? _____
Assistant: _____
Partner: _____
_____
_____

When? _____
Assistant: _____
Partner: _____
_____
_____

How? _____
Assistant: _____
Partner: _____
_____
_____

Tongue Twisters!

Warm-up

Tongue twisters are tricky, but they can help us practice pronunciation.

What is a tongue twister from your language?

_____

_____

_____

_____

Activity

Let's ask our digital assistant for a tongue twister.
Listen carefully! Practice speaking the tongue twister you heard by saying it aloud. Then, write it out here:

_____

_____

_____

Here are some more tongue twisters.
Try speaking them aloud now with a partner.

- *Fuzzy Wuzzy was a bear. Fuzzy Wuzzy had no hair. Fuzzy Wuzzy wasn't fuzzy, was he?*
- *How many cookies could a good cook cook, if a good cook could cook cookies?*
- *I saw a kitten eating chicken in the kitchen.*
- *I scream, you scream, we all scream for ice cream.*
- *If a dog chews shoes, whose shoes does he choose?*
- *Four fine fresh fish for free.*
- *Fred fed Ted bread, and Ted fed Fred bread.*
- *She sells seashells by the seashore.*

Practice

Get into teams of five, and make your own tongue-twisters.
For each person:

1. On a piece of paper, write your first name. (Pass the paper to the person on your right).
2. Write down something that he/she did. (Pass the paper to the person on your right).
3. Write down where he/she did it. (Pass the paper to the person on your right).
4. Write down when he/she did it. (Pass the paper to the person on your right).
5. Write down the reason why he/she did it. (Pass the paper to the person on your right).

This will give your group five tongue twisters.
For example,

* *David drank a drink in downtown Denpasar at daylight to destress*
* *Noddy needed noodles in Neverland at noon to 'nom nom nom'*

You might need to ask the digital assistant to help you create your tongue twister.
Ask questions like:

* *What are some actions that begin with the letter [...]?*
* *What are place names that begin with the letter [...]?*
* *What are emotions that begin with the letter [...]?*

Further practice

1. Ask the digital assistant to repeat your tongue twister after you. See if it can repeat it the same way, or if you can trick it.
   Did you trick it? Yes or No.

2. Hear some more tongue twisters. Ask the digital assistant to tell you some more tongue twisters. Write down the tongue twisters that you hear.

   a) _____
   _____
   _____
   _____

   b) _____
   _____
   _____
   _____

   c) _____
   _____
   _____
   _____

   d) _____
   _____
   _____
   _____

   e) _____
   _____
   _____
   _____

15
Resources list

As sites continuously go down, merge, and emerge, perhaps only a small selection of all appropriate resource content should be presented here. An attempt at keeping the number of resources to a select few for each type also provides a sample that is both comprehensive and extensive, but not overwhelming. Like any other instructor resource list, individuals will be able to add to the content as they find material that is useful, create their own bookmark list, and over time, curate a vast resource library tailored to their individual teaching and learning context. Each section of this list is broken down into applications most of which are freely available for use with Android or iOS devices, computers, or web-based platforms.

Teachers who wish to make notes, or to record any additional resources that they come across, can use the notes section at the end of this chapter.

The following content is covered:

- App creation
- Audio creation/editing
- Blogs
- Bookmarking
- Books
- Chatbots
- Coding
- Comic strip generators
- Copyright
- Digital assistant actions and skills (development and listings)
- Digital assistants
- Digital story creation
- Image resources
- Image editing
- Interactive whiteboards
- Mashups
- Media timelines
- Music resources
- Podcasting
- Podcatchers
- Presentations
- Publishing
- QR codes
- Rubrics
- Screencasting
- Storyboarding and scripting
- Story creation apps
- Voice-assisted language learning
- Video editing
- Video resources
- WebQuests
- Wikis

App Creation
Android – n/a
iOS – n/a
Computer – n/a
Web

> *Android Creator* [free/paid] creates free Android apps without the need for programming knowledge.
>
> *AppMakr* [free/paid] is a template-based application creator that relies on the drag and drop of elements for the development of no-coding-required applications. It is available in a variety of languages.
>
> *Appy Pie* [free/paid] relies on templates as well as drag and drop for users to begin creating their app. It requires no coding skills.
>
> *AppYourself* [paid] is an app creation tool aimed at the business market.
>
> *Como DIY* [paid] is a do-it-yourself app creation tool aimed to mostly target to businesses, and is available in a number of languages.
>
> *iBuildApp* [paid] is a template driven app creator for iPhone and Android phones.

Audio Creation/Editing
Android

> *PCM Recorder* [free] is a simple voice recorder.
>
> *Pocket WavePad* [free] records edits and adds effects to audio.
>
> *TapeMachine* [paid] is a graphical sound recorder and editor.

iOS

Pocket WavePad [free] records edits and adds effects to audio.

Voice Memos [paid] is voice recorder that allows multitasking.

Computer

Audacity [free] is an open source digital editing program available for Mac and PC which you can use to record, edit, and mix narration and music.

Pocket WavePad [free] records, edits, and adds effects to audio for Mac.

GoldWave [free/paid] is a digital audio editor that provides simple recording as well as more sophisticated processing, restoration, enhancement, and conversion for Windows and Linux. A free version is available for evaluation purposes, after which a lifetime license can be purchased.

Web

Twistedwave [free] is a browser-based audio editor that can record or edit any audio file.

Blogs

Android

Blogaway [free] is a simple application to allow blogging on the go. It works with Blogger and allows for post creation, adding of photos, videos, multiple account management, saving of drafts, bookmarking, and a host of formatting options.

iOS

Disqus [free] is a commenting system that can be included in blogs as an add-on. The application provides an easy way to moderate comments and publish responses to keep engagement levels high.

TravelPod – Travel Blog [free] is a blogging application that works on- and offline, and is designed to be used while traveling.

Computer – n/a

Web

Blogger.com [free] will host your blog for free, and aside from being very easy to use, it allows some level of privacy so that it can be suitable for use as a class blogging site. From a single account, you can create as many blogs as you wish and determine who is allowed to comment on the content.

BuzzSumo [paid] allows users to search for blog posts that have been highly shared across social media.

Edublogs.org [free] allows teachers to create and manage their own and students' websites. There is room for customization of design and the ability to add various media to this private and secure platform.

Kidblog.org [free] is an easy-to-use, safe, and secure publishing platform designed for students in grades K-12. There are a number of excellent features including privacy and password protection, and there is no need for student personal information to be collected, nor is there any advertising. It is free for up to fifty students per class.

WordPress.org [free] is one of the most popular blogging platforms in use today as it is open- source and is easily customizable. The downloadable software for self-hosting purposes is much more flexible than that available on the blogging platform. *Twitter* [free] deserves a mention here as it is useful for microblogging (posting short frequent updates). It allows users to post and read short 140-character posts called 'tweets'.

Tumblr [free] is a blogging platform open to those over thirteen years of age, with most users using pen names over their real names when blogging. Users can post on their blog, follow others, and search posts. It is unique in that posts are divided into media types: text, photo, quote, link, chat, audio, and video.

Bookmarking
Android

Bookmark [free] is a cross-platform app that allows for the syncing of bookmarks across different browsers and devices.

Delicious [free] provides users with the ability to organize links to content on the internet that they would like to save, the ability to discover links, edit tags and comments, and also to explore content saved by friends.

Facebook Save [free] is a built-in option for saving Facebook news content to read at a later date.

Instapaper [free] provides an offline archiving solution for web pages, and it presents this content to be read in newspaper fashion. Content can be highlighted, and notes can be added while reading.

Pinterest [free] allows users to pin posts (for example, web pages, images, and videos) and organize them around a common theme.

Pocket [free] integrates with a large number of third party applications that allow for the building of bookmarks. Web pages, videos, images, and whatever else can be used offline for bookmarking. Archiving maintains the links but removes the content from offline availability.

iOS

Delicious [free] allows users to save content from the internet (including web pages, blog posts, tweets, pictures, and video), and provides options for searching through others' collections of links.

Facebook Save [free] is a built-in option for saving Facebook news content to read at a later date.

Instapaper [free] provides an offline archiving solution for web pages and presents this content to be read in newspaper fashion. Content can be highlighted, and notes can be added while reading.

Pinterest [free] allows users to pin posts (for example, web pages, images, and videos) and organize them around a common theme.

Pocket [free] integrates with a large number of third party applications that allow for the building of bookmarks. Web pages, videos, images, and whatever else can be used offline for bookmarking. Archiving maintains the links but removes the content from offline availability.

Computer

EdwinSoft's UltimateDemon [paid] is link building software that helps to provide search engine optimization to a website.

Pinterest [free] allows users to pin posts (for example, web pages, images, and videos) and organize them around a common theme.

Pocket [free] integrates with a large number of third party applications that allow for the building of bookmarks. Web pages, videos, images, and whatever else can be used offline for bookmarking. Archiving maintains the links but removes the content from offline availability.

ReadKit [trial/paid] offers an Apple Mac curative and archiving platform for the content found in your other bookmarking applications (like Pocket and Instapaper) and RSS readers. It also provides an extra level of organization to this content.

Web

Delicious [free] is a social bookmarking site that allows users to bookmark webpages to the internet instead of locally.

Facebook Save [free] is a built-in option for saving Facebook news content to read at a later date.

Instapaper [free] provides an offline archiving solution for web pages, and it presents this content to be read in newspaper fashion. Content can be highlighted, and notes can be added while reading.

OnlyWire [paid] works with WordPress and offers automatic submission of content to social networking and social bookmarking sites.

Pocket [free] integrates with a large number of third party applications that allow for the building of bookmarks. Web pages, videos, images, and whatever else can be used offline for bookmarking. Archiving maintains the links but removes the content from offline availability.

Books
Android
Wattpad Free Books [free] provides access to free stories and books written by aspiring authors.
iOS
Free Books – Ultimate Classics Library [free] features free access to 23,469 classic books.
Computer – n/a
Web
BookRix [free] allows access to thousands of books to read either online or to download as ebooks.

Children's Storybooks Online [free] provides a series of illustrated stories for all ages to read.

Chatbots
Android
Mitsuki [free] is a chatterbot that simulates an 18-year-old female, and is considered to be the most human-like AI. It has won the Loebner Prize Turing Test four times.

Mydol [free] is a chatbot that allows you to hold conversations with a virtual version of celebrities.

Poncho [free] is a weather bot that provides daily forecasts and alerts. It can also be accessed via Facebook Messenger, Viber, Kik, and Slack.

Replika [free] is a chatbot that serves as a personal friend, and one that you can have conversations with regarding daily life (and its ups and downs).

Wysa [free] is a chatbot designed to help people deal with mental health issues, including anxiety, stress, and depression.

iOS

Mydol [free] is a chatbot that allows you to hold conversations with virtual versions of celebrities.

Replika [free] is a chatbot that serves as a personal friend, and one that you can have conversations with regarding daily life (and its ups and downs).

Virtual Talk – AI Chatbot [free] is a chatbot that simulates whoever you wish to talk to, such as a famous person or celebrity.

Wysa [free] is a chatbot designed to help people deal with mental health issues, including anxiety, stress, and depression.

Computer – n/a

Web

A.L.I.C.E [free] is the Artificial Linguistic Internet Computer Entity. It is a natural language processing chatbot which relies upon heuristic pattern matching rules when receiving human input.

Amy (x.ai) [free] is a personal assistant that can schedule meetings, and is accessible by CCing it in an email. Taking into consideration schedules, locations, and preferences, the chatbot will respond with suggestions for the perfect meeting time.

Chatbots.org [free] is a website dedicated to providing a listing of available chatbots, virtual agents, virtual assistants, conversation agents, and so on. Detailed information and a link to each are provided.

Hello Hipmunk [free] is a personal travel assistant that can assist with booking flights and hotels. It is available on various platforms including Facebook Messenger, Skype, and Slack, and it also integrates into email and your calendar. Similar to *Amy (x.ai)*, it can also be added to email threads for collaborative travel planning.

Mitsuki [free] is a chatterbot that simulates an 18-year-old female, and is considered to be the most human-like AI. It has won the Loebner Prize Turing Test four times.

Replika [free] is a chatbot that serves as a personal friend, and one that you can have conversations with regarding daily life (and its ups and downs).

Wysa [free] is a chatbot designed to help people deal with mental health issues, including anxiety, stress, and depression.

Zo [free] is a social chatbot for entertainment. It was created by Microsoft.

Coding
Android

Run Marco! [free] offers users the opportunity to play an adventure game while they learn to code. The application presents instructions using 'Blocky', which is the same as that used by the official Hour of Code tutorials.

Tynker [free] is an easy way for children to learn programming skills as they solve puzzles to learn concepts and build games, or control robots and drones. A number of templates are available for free.

iOS

Codea [paid] is a software development tool that uses the Lua programming language to teach users how to program.

Hopscotch [free] is an application that allows users to begin learning to code by making games similar to Angry Birds, and sharing them so others can play them.

ScratchJr [free] allows users to program their own interactive stories and games by snapping together graphical programming blocks. The application was inspired by the Scratch programming language.

Tynker [free] is an easy way for children to learn programming skills as they solve puzzles to learn concepts and build games, or control robots and drones. A number of templates are available for free.

Computer

Scratch [free] allows users to create stories, games, and animations using the Scratch programming language, and then share these with others. It is a project of the Lifelong Kindergarten Group at the MIT Media Lab.

Lightbot – Programming Puzzles [paid] is an OS X game-based application that allows players to use programming logic to solve levels. The app is also available for Android and iOS devices.

Web – n/a

Comic Strip Generators

Android

Comic Maker [free] creates comics from the photo gallery.

Comic Strip It! Lite [free] takes photos or use photo gallery images to create a comic.

iOS

Comic Life 3 [paid] turns photos into comic pages, or creates an entire comic from scratch using templates to build pages with speech balloons, comic lettering, and photo filters.

ToonTastic [free] is a wizard-based animated comic or cartoon creator.

Strip Designer [paid] is software for comic creation that uses camera, library, or Facebook photo options to create a comic.

Computer

Comic Creator [paid] is a basic template driven comic creator for use on a Windows computer.

Web

Pixton [free/paid] is an easy to use comprehensive online comic creator that supports narration, and offers a range of signup options from a free fun option to paid educator/business accounts.

MakeBeliefsComix [free] is a basic comic creator that uses black and white images over a four-panel comic strip. An iOS version is also available.

Toonlet [free] allows for anyone to create their own cartoon characters and web comics.

Toondoo [free] allows for the drag and drop creation of comic strips. An iOS version is also available.

Copyright
Android – n/a
iOS – n/a
Computer – n/a
Web

> *Creative Commons Licenses* [free] gives detailed information regarding the various types of licensing afforded to creative commons, and the permissions that each license grants for the use specific works.
>
> *Image Codr* [free] can assist learners and teachers alike in determining how a Flickr image can be used (as determined by the original photographer), and provides users with an automatically generated Creative Commons citation regarding the images use within digital projects.

Digital Assistant Actions and Skills (development and listings)
Android – *n/a*
Computer – *n/a*
iOS – *n/a*

Web

Alexa Skills [free] is a listing of all the available Skills for use with Alexa. Each listing is available by category, and provides information on how to utilize the Skill.

Alexa Blueprints [free] allows you to create personal Alexa skills, using a variety of templates, to develop flash card and trivia-based games through to customizations that can help extend the functionality of Alexa across devices such as the Echo smart speaker.

Actions on Google [free] allows you to create personal Google Assistant Actions using a variety of templates from flash cards and trivia-based games along with other actions to extend the functionality, of the Google Assistant across devices such as the Google Home smart speaker.

Google Assistant Actions [free] is a listing of all the actions available for the Google Assistant. Each listing is available by category or search, and provides information about the skill as well as on what devices and platforms it can be used.

Invocable [free/paid] uses a block-based design to help users create a voice user interface and skills for Alexa.

Story Speaker [free] is one of the many existing Google Assistant voice experiments. It is a Chrome extension that allows you to use a Google Document to write a choose-your-own adventure story that plays as an interactive talking story.

Voiceflow [free/paid] is an easy to use, intuitive, code free way to prototype and publish Alexa skills using a drag and drop interface.

Digital Assistants
Android

Alexa [free/paid] was developed by Amazon with an initial release in November of 2014. Alexa can be found in devices such as the Amazon range of smart speakers. The wake-word can be set by the user, with the default being *Alexa*. The assistant is also as an application for smartphones and tablets.

Google Assistant [free/paid] was developed by Google with an initial release in May of 2016. It is primarily accessible on mobile and smart home devices as well as Google smartphones and Android devices including Wear OS, it is also available as a stand-alone application for iOS, and integrated within Android Auto. The wake-phrases for the assistant include "Hey, Google", and "OK, Google".

iOS

Alexa [free/paid] was developed by Amazon with an initial release in November of 2014. Alexa can be found in devices such as the Amazon range of smart speakers. The wake-word can be set by the user, with the default being *Alexa*. The assistant is also as an application for smartphones and tablets.

Siri [free/paid] was developed by Apple Inc. with a release in October of 2011. Siri is the virtual assistant that became part of iOS, watchOS, MacOs, the HomePod and the tvOS operating systems. As an application it was initially released in February of 2010 for iOS. It can also be accessed through the latest version of the MacOS and Apple CarPlay. The wake-phrase for this assistant is "Hey, Siri".

Computer

Cortana [free/paid] was developed by Microsoft with an initial release in April of 2014. Cortana is the virtual assistant for Windows 10 and other related Microsoft products (including smartphones, tablets, Xbox, band fitness tracker, surface headphones, Windows mixed reality). It also runs on the Invoke smart speaker, Android, and iOS. If always-listening mode has been selected in Windows 10, then the wake-phrase 'Hey, Cortana" can be used to activate the assistant.

Siri [free/paid] was developed by Apple Inc. with a release in October of 2011. Siri is the virtual assistant that became part of iOS, watchOS, MacOs, the HomePod and the tvOS operating systems. As an application it was initially released in February of 2010 for iOS. It can also be accessed through the latest version of the MacOS and Apple CarPlay. The wake-phrase for this assistant is "Hey, Siri".

Web

Alexa [free/paid] was developed by Amazon with an initial release in November of 2014. Alexa can be found in devices such as the Amazon range of smart speakers. The wake-word can be set by the user, with the default being *Alexa*. The assistant is also as an application for smartphones and tablets.

Cortana [free/paid] was developed by Microsoft with an initial release in April of 2014. Cortana is the virtual assistant for Windows 10 and other related Microsoft products (including smartphones, tablets, Xbox, band fitness tracker, surface headphones, Windows mixed reality). It also runs on the Invoke smart speaker, Android, and iOS. If always-listening mode has been selected in Windows 10, then the wake-phrase 'Hey, Cortana" can be used to activate the assistant.

Google Assistant [free/paid] was developed by Google with an initial release in May of 2016. It is primarily accessible on mobile and smart home devices as well as Google smartphones and Android devices including Wear OS, it is also available as a stand-alone application for iOS, and integrated within Android Auto. The wake-phrases for the assistant include "Hey, Google", and "OK, Google".

Siri [free/paid] was developed by Apple Inc. with a release in October of 2011. Siri is the virtual assistant that became part of iOS, watchOS, MacOs, the HomePod and the tvOS operating systems. As an application it was initially released in February of 2010 for iOS. It can also be accessed through the latest version of the MacOS and Apple CarPlay. The wake-phrase for this assistant is "Hey, Siri".

Digital Story Creation
Android

Com-Phone Story Maker [free] combines audio, photos, and text to create stories while allowing for three different layers of audio.

WeVideo [free] is a web-based video editor that can mix images, text, video, and audio.

iOS

30hands [free] creates a story by adding narration to photos.

Magisto [free] uses a wizard to create a short video based on provided images or video content.

Splice [free/paid] combines photos, videos, music and narrations. Effects and transitions can be added.

WeVideo [free] is a web-based video editor that can mix images, text, video, and audio.

Computer

iMovie [paid] provides video creation and editing software that can create easily shareable content on a Mac. An iOS version is available.

Microsoft Photo Story 3 [free] for Windows lets you create slideshows from a wizard that includes audio, narration, and images.

Windows Movie Maker [free] for Windows operating systems is a video editing software application that allows for narration, audio, images, and video to be mixed and edited, and it comes with transitions and special effects.

Web

Animoto [paid] allows users to submit songs, choose a theme, add their photos, videos, and text to create a digital story that they can share.

Meograph [free] is a digital storytelling tool that relies on Google Earth to create map-based and timeline-based narrated stories.

WeVideo [free] is a web-based video editor that can mix images, text, video, and audio.

Image Resources

Android – n/a

iOS – n/a

Computer – n/a

Web

Cagle Cartoons [free] provides access to a number of political cartoons from around the world. The images are organized by topic with artists categorized by country.

Flickr Creative Commons [free] provides images that can be used for almost any educational project, as long as proper citation is followed

FreeFoto.com [free] has a photos area that is available under three licensing options: recognition, Creative Commons, and commercial.

Morguefile [free] provides a range of images that are copyright free, and are available for use with few or no restrictions.

Pics4Learning.com [free] is a website that provides safe and free images for educational uses. Images here are copyright-friendly and can be used for classrooms, multimedia projects, websites, videos, portfolios, or other projects.

PicSearch [free] allows you to search the internet for images, but be aware that the image may not be copyright-free, or that it may require permission to be used in projects or in any other educational contexts.

The Library of Congress Prints & Photographs Online Catalog [free] makes an attempt to ensure that as many of their images as possible are available online in a digital format.

Wikimedia [free] serves as a point from where all the images and video posted in Wikipedia can be viewed. Most of the images found here are either copyright-free or free for use with minimal restrictions.

Image Editing
Android

PicSay [free] can edit photos, overlay titles, and add special effects.

FX Camera [free] is a photo booth app that allows users to add various effects to photographs.

iOS

PhotoPad [free] can create, edit, and save vector illustrations. It can also work with photo library images.

ScreenChomp [free] allows you to share, explain, and markup images.

Computer

PhotoPad [paid] is an image editor for OS X.

PaintShop Pro [paid] is a comprehensive image editing package for Windows.

Web

Adobe Photoshop CC [paid] is a comprehensive cloud-based image editing package.

Phixr [free] is an online photo editor with various filters and effects, and it can connect to various social media sites.

FotoFlexer [free] is an online image editor offering a number of effects, distortions, and other features.

Pixlr [paid] is a comprehensive online photo editing app.

Interactive Whiteboards

Android

ExplainEverything [free] allows users to share their content by using an interactive screencasting whiteboard.

Interactive Whiteboard [free] is a virtual whiteboard that can be used for drawing or teaching various concepts as it allows for multiple finger input, straight line drawing mode, drawing move mode, and various other features.

PPT and Whiteboard Sharing [free] provides a way to share presentations, videos, and drawings in various settings including the classroom, the boardroom, and online meetings.

Whiteboard: Collaborative Draw [free] is a collaborative drawing application that allows real-time painting.

iOS

Doceri [trial/paid] combines screencasting, desktop control, and an interactive whiteboard in one application, with control through Airplay or through Mac or PC.

Educreations Interactive Whiteboard [free] is an interactive whiteboard and screencasting tool that allows annotation, animation, and narration of a number of content types.

Screenchomp [free] allows users to annotate pictures or to use the application as a whiteboard. Any work completed with the application can be saved automatically to the internet.

ShowMe Interactive Whiteboard [free] allows voice-over recording of whiteboard interactions so that tutorials can be created easily before being shared online.

Computer

Open Sakore [free] is open-source and it is dedicated to teacher and student use. It allows for insertion of multiple document types, along with annotation capabilities for commenting drawing and highlighting content.

Smoothboard Air [free] is a collaborative interactive whiteboard for multiple iPads and for Android tablets. It allows users to annotate desktop applications wirelessly through the use of a web browser.

Web

A Web Whiteboard [free] is a online whiteboard application that allows a number of devices (like computers, tablets, and smartphones), to draw sketches, and to collaborate with others around the globe.

Realtime Board [free] is a whiteboard in a browser that allows for collaboration among a number of users.

Twiddla [free] is a web-based meeting environment that allows users to mark up photos, graphics, and websites, or to just start out with a blank canvas.

Web Whiteboard [free] is a simple way to draw and write together online by creating an online whiteboard with a click, and sharing it live or by sending the link to others.

Mashups

Android

Edjing 5 DJ Music Mixer [free] not only transforms any android device into a turntable, but it provides access to a range of music libraries.

iOS

iMashup [paid] is a professional quality remixing app that allows users to create their own mashups and remixes.

Pacemaker [free] allows users to create and save mixes on an iPhone or iWatch, and to DJ live from iPad devices.

Computer

Mixxx [free] is an advanced open source DJ package that includes an extensive array of features for OS X and Windows.

Web

Mashstix [free] is a website with user submitted mashups available.

Media Timelines

Android

RWT Timelines [free] allows students to create a graphical representation of any event or process by displaying items sequentially along a line. The final product can be exported as a pdf, or saved to the device's camera roll.

Timeline [free] allows users to create timelines and associate them with colors, and to view multiple timelines together. It is a useful reference tool for remembering dates.

iOS

TimelineBuilder [paid] allows users to create custom timelines with images and text with unique beginning and end dates.

Timeline Maker [free] provides an easy way to display a series of events in a chronological order.

Computer

Edraw Timeline Maker [paid] is a tool that makes it simple to create a professional looking timeline, history, schedule, time table, or project plan diagram from scratch.

TimelineMaker [paid] provides a simplified timeline charting tool aimed at project planners, and business professionals, and those in educational contexts.

Web

Capzles [free] allows users to create rich multimedia experiences from videos, photos, music, blogs, and documents by integrating these into a timeline of sequential events, and then share them on various social media platforms.

Hstry [free] is specifically designed for the education sector, and it allows teachers and students to create interactive timelines for assignments and online sharing.

OurStory [free] offers a means for creating story-based timelines with pictures.

Timeline [free] from *readwritethink* allows students of all ages to easily create a graphical representation of related items or events in sequential order and display them along a line using various images and text.

TimeGlider [free] is a web-based timeline project creator that allows zooming and panning across timelines. Users are able to set the size of events as they relate to importance.

Tiki-Toki [free/paid] is a web-based timeline editor that allows viewing of timelines in 3D, and it allows for the integration of images and videos.

WhenInTime [free] is a web application for creating and sharing media-based timelines.

Music Resources
Android
FindSounds [free] can be used to search the internet for sounds that can then be saved as ringtones, notifications, or alarms.

Shazam [free] allows Android device users to identify the music playing around them, as well as discover song lyrics, and other music related information and tracks.

iOS
Shazam [free] allows iOS device users to identify the music playing around them, as well as discover song lyrics, and other music related information and tracks.

Computer – n/a
Web
300 Monks [free] provides a comprehensive source of royalty free music.

ccMixter [free] is a free music site that is community based and promotes a remix culture. *A cappella* and remix tracks licensed under Creative Commons are available for download and use in creative works.

FMA (Free Music Archive) [free] provides access to a range of free music based on a wide variety of genre. The music is offered free under various licenses for use.

Find Sounds [free] is a long-running service that can be used to search the internet for various sounds that can then be incorporated into various projects.

FreePlay Music [free] is a service that searches the internet for free music that can be used in YouTube videos and other projects.

Podcasting
Android

Podomatic Podcast & Mix Player [free] provides access to a wide variety of podcasts, listening in offline mode, and features such as a dynamic social feed so you can see the podcasts Facebook friends follow and like.

iOS

PodOmatic Podcast Player [free] provides access to a wide variety of podcasts, listening in offline mode, and features such as a dynamic social feed so you can see the podcasts Facebook friends follow and like.

Computer

Audacity [free] is a free multi-track audio recorder and editor with some very powerful features that include those for adding effects to files and conducting analysis of the audio recorded.

iTunes [free] offers media on demand and a way to organize and enjoy music, movies, and TV shows, as well as accessing and subscribing to podcasts and screencasts.

LoudBlog [free] is a Content Manager System (CMS) for podcasts. This program automatically generates skinnable websites and RSS-feeds for audio and video podcasts, including provision for show notes and links.

PodcastGenerator [free] is an open source content management system for podcast publishing. It provides a comprehensive range of tools to manage all aspects of podcast publishing.

PodProducer [free] allows for the recording of voice and the adding of effects.

Web

ESLPod [free] provides a range of podcast content tailored to second-language learners of English from specific topics through to test-taking guides.

FeedForAll [free] allows for the creation, editing, and publishing of RSS feeds.

Feedity [free] is an online tool for creating an RSS feed for any web page, with an option to upgrade to a premium account that offers additional features.

FETCHRSS: RSS Generator [free] is an online RSS feed generator, that can create a feed out of almost any web page, automatically updates the RSS feed when new content is added to the web page, and generates an RSS for a social networking site.

OPML Viewer [free] allows users to view the contents of outline processor markup language (OPML) files.

Podcast Alley [free] is the place to go if you are interested in podcasts, want to gain access to the top podcasts, and want to find out the latest news about podcasts.

Pod Gallery [free] is a podcasting website where podcasters can share their episodes, and where listeners can subscribe.

QT-ESL Podcasts [free] provides a range of podcasts that cover oral grammar practice and includes scripts and worksheets.

SoundCloud [free] is a social sound platform where anyone is able to create and share audio.

Podcatchers
Android

Podcast Player [free] provides a range of podcast discovery options and tools, along with a range of features including a sleep timer, video support, intelligent silence skip and volume boost, as well as support for tablet, Chromecast, and Android Wear.

Podcast Republic [free] is an application that is ad-supported. It offers a variety of features from podcast discovery and automatic downloading through to storage management, sleep timer, and car mode. Support is also included from Chromecast and Android Wear.

Pocket Casts [paid] shows subscribed podcasts in a tile format, with easy sorting and categorization functions. Video podcast is also supported, along with auto-download and cleanup of downloaded and played episodes to save on storage space. Several features allow it to stand out, including a sleep timer as well as its cross-platform nature that grants it the ability to sync between multiple devices and mobile operating systems.

iOS

Overcast: Podcast Player [free] provides a combination of powerful audio and podcast management features. The application comes with a wide variety of features that allow it to download episodes, send notifications of new episodes, and play content offline or by streaming. It can also normalize speech levels, and speed through gaps and silence in podcasts.

Castro: High Fidelty Podcasts [free] is a simple and easy to use podcatcher. It provides a simple design with automatic episode download, dynamic storage management, along with episode streaming.

Pocket Casts [paid] shows subscribed podcasts in a tile format, with easy sorting and categorization functions. Video podcast is also supported, along with auto-download and cleanup of downloaded and played episodes to save on storage space. Several features allow it to stand out, including a sleep timer as well as its cross-platform nature that grants it the ability to sync between multiple devices and mobile operating systems.

Computer

gPodder [free] is an open source media aggregator and podcast client. It is able to store information in the cloud on which shows you have listened to, and it allows for the local installation of the client for download of content.

iTunes [free] is a comprehensive media aggregator that provides comprehensive support for media management, the audio and video playback of local media, podcast search and subscription, along with automatic downloads, syncing and streaming, and many other features.

Juice [free] is a long-standing cross platform no-frills podcast aggregator that is open source, and specifically designed to manage podcasts. Features include auto cleanup, centralized feed management, and for Windows users, accessibility options for the blind and visually impaired.

Web

Cloud Caster [free] is a web-based podcaster which works across all mobile devices. It syncs progress and playlists across platforms, and provides search and support for audio and video podcasts.

Presentations

Android

Glogster [free] allows students using an Android-based device to create online multimedia posters, or Glogs, from a combination of media types (from audio, graphic, to video), and hyperlinks.

Google Slides [free] allows Android device users with a Google account a means of creating, editing, and collaborating with others on presentations.

LinkedIn SlideShare [free] allows Android device users the ability to search and explore for a variety of presentations, infographics, and documents on topics of their interest.

Microsoft PowerPoint [free] allows users to view PowerPoint presentations on their device for free, and to make edits and changes on the go.

iOS

Glogster [free] allows students using an iOS device to create online multimedia posters, or Glogs, from a combination of media types (from audio, graphic, to video), and hyperlinks.

Google Slides [free] allows iOS device users with a Google account a means of creating, editing, and collaborating with others on presentations.

Keynote [free] is a powerful presentation app that allows users to develop comprehensive presentations with animations, transitions, and multimedia elements.

LinkedIn SlideShare [free] allows iOS device users the ability to search and explore for a variety of presentations, infographics, and documents on topics of their interest.

Microsoft PowerPoint [free] allows users to view PowerPoint presentations on their device for free, and to make edits and changes on the go.

Computer

Microsoft PowerPoint [paid] is a comprehensive presentation software application, and is perhaps the most used and recognizable.

Keynote [free] is a powerful presentation app that allows users to develop comprehensive presentations with animations, transitions, and multimedia elements.

Web

Bunkr [free] is a presentation tool that displays any online content including social media posts, images, videos, audio, articles, and files.

Glogster [free] allows students to create online multimedia posters, or Glogs, from a combination of media types (from audio, graphic, to video), and hyperlinks.

Google Slides [free] allows those with a Google account, a means of creating, editing, and collaborating with others on presentations.

LinkedIn SlideShare [free] allows users to search for presentations, infographics, documents and other items on topics of their interest.

Microsoft PowerPoint Online [free] extends the Microsoft PowerPoint experience to the web browser with OneDrive integration, and allows users to create, edit, and view files on the go.

Prezi [free] is a visually oriented presentation packaged that also allows users to upload PowerPoint slides, and customize them, or use a variety of their own images, text, audio, and video.

Slidebean [free] offers a one-click presentation development system that incorporates a variety of templates into the design of presentations.

Slides [free] is a place for creating, presenting, and sharing slide decks.

Swipe [free] allows users to share a presentation link with anyone across any device, and it allows viewers to interact with the presentation on several levels, from collaboration through to taking polls.

VoiceThread [free] allows users to import various media such as images, PowerPoints, and PDFs. It provides a means of making audio or video recordings concerning those media artifacts, and it also allows other users to reply to the initial comments, by audio or video means, as the presentation progresses.

Publishing
Android

Book Creator Free [free] offers a simple means of creating a variety of ebooks including picture books, comic and photo books, and journals and textbooks. It allows for the use of images, narration, texts, annotations and drawings.

Book Writer Free [free] is a simple book creation application that allows users to share their content with others.

My Story Builder [free] is a simple, 'suitable for children', book editor.

Scribble: Kids Book Maker [paid] is an application that allows children to write, illustrate, and publish their own comprehensive stories in a range of formations including video export. It contains a series of story starters, stickers, and backgrounds to help them work on creating stories from the start.

iOS

Book Creator Free [free] offers a simple means of creating a variety of ebooks including picture books, comic and photo books, and journals and textbooks. It allows for the use of images, narration, texts, annotations and drawings.

Creative Book Builder [paid] is a professional ebook editor and generator which can also extend the utility of ebooks through the use of a range of widgets.

Demibooks Composer Pro [free] builds interactive books with animation, audio, images, and effects.

Scribble Press – Creative Book Maker for Kids [paid] contains a series of story starters, stickers and backgrounds to help get young kids working on creating stories that can be turned into ebooks.

Computer

Android Book App Maker [paid] provides users with the ability to turn content into a flip-book app.

iBooks Author [free] provides a series of templates and styles to assist in the development of ebooks for the iBook store.

Kotobee [free] provides free software to assist in the creation of ebooks and libraries for a range of platforms.

Web

Blurb [paid] is just one of many online services that can assist in the creation of ebooks.

QR Codes

Android

I-nigma QR & Barcode Scanner (free) is a versatile barcode and QR code reader that can scan a multitude of codes and share these codes as well.

QR Code Reader (free) is a simple QR Code and product barcode scanner.

QR Droid Code Scanner (free) is a powerful barcode, QR code, and Data Matrix scanner that offers multi-language support.

iOS

Bakodo – Barcode Scanner and QR Barcode Reader (free) scans all types of QR codes and barcodes.

QR Reader for iPhone (free) scans a variety of codes including QR codes and barcodes, and features auto-detect scanning.

QRafter – QR Code and Barcode Reader and Generator (free) is a two-dimensional barcode scanner for iOS. Along with a variety of useful features, it can scan and generate QR codes.

Computer

CodeTwo QR Code Desktop Reader (free) allows users to scan QR codes directly from their screen onto their desktop. Users select the QR code to be read by selecting the area with a QR code using their mouse.

QR-Code Studio (free) is for Mac and Windows computers. The QR code maker software is freeware.

Web

QR Code Generator (free) creates QR codes, in a limited number of formats, for free.

QR Stuff QR Code Generator (free) creates QR codes from a various types of data such as website URLs, image files, PDF files, and so on, with static and dynamic embedding options.

The QR Code Generator (free) allows for the free scan and generation of QR codes for a variety of uses.

Rubrics

Android

Daily Rubric: Any Curriculum [free] allows teachers to create and use rubrics from their Android device.

Rubrics can be designed from curriculum outcomes, or based on the pre-loaded Common Core Standards.

iOS

Easy Assessment [paid] offers a means to capture and assess performance based on custom created rubrics, scale, or criteria.

Rubrics [paid] allows instructors to track student performance and produce reports based on custom rubrics and grading options.

Computer – n/a

Web

Kathy Shrock's Guide to Everything: Assessment and Rubrics [free] provides access to a wide range of rubrics to help guide assessment of students.

iRubric [free] is a website where instructors can create their own rubrics, or they can build off those made available from other instructors.

RubiStar [free] allows instructors to create their own rubrics using templates designed for core subjects as well as art, music, and multimedia.

Screencasting

Android

AZ Screen Recorder [free] is a screen recording application that offers several features, including the ability to capture the front camera as well as screen recording. It also provides video trimming.

ilos Screen Recorder [free] is a simple application that records the screen and provides audio capture as well.

Telecine [free] is an open source application that allows screen recording through the use of overlays.

iOS

Doceri [trial/paid] combines screencasting, desktop control, and an interactive whiteboard in one application, with control through Airplay or through Mac or PC.

Educreations Interactive Whiteboard [free] is an interactive whiteboard and screencasting tool that allows annotation, animation, and narration of a number of content types.

Screenchomp [free] allows users to annotate pictures or to use the application as a whiteboard. Any work completed with the application can be saved automatically to the internet.

Computer

ilos screen recorder [free] automatically uploads content to their servers for storage and playback.

Screencast-O-Matic [free] offers fifteen minutes of recording time for free, both for screen and webcam, and allows users to save to places such as YouTube or as a video file.

TechSmith Camtasia Studio [free trial] is a comprehensive screen recording application that allows for audio and webcam capture as well as highlighting, adding media, and editing of recordings.

Web – n/a

Storyboarding and Scripting

Android

Ray Story Board [free] is a simple storyboard creator that lets users build storyboards from photos or gallery images, create multiple storyboards, and animate them using a slideshow feature.

Storyboard Studio [paid] is a mobile storyboarding writing tool that is suitable for artists and non-artists alike.

iOS

Penultimate [free] provides a natural feel of writing and sketching on paper, and connects to Evernote.

Storyboard Composer [paid] is a mobile storyboard previsualiztion composer for animators, art directors, film students, film directors, or anyone who would like to visualize their story.

Computer

FrameForge Previz Studio [paid] allows users to develop and previsualize films, TV shows, commercials, or similar projects at a professional level.

Storyboardpro [paid] is professional level software that combines drawing and animation tools with camera controls.

StoryBoard Quick Studio [paid] allows for the fast creation of storyboards with QuickShots, has a print-to-sketch feature, and comes with a series of character poses for integration into storylines.

Web

Google Docs [free] can be used, along with any note-taking or document editor, as a make-shift storyboard by integrating photos or pictures into the document to outline a process or the actions for a story. It is also available as an Android and iOS app.

StoryboardThat [free trial] offers an edition that allows educators to build diagrams, and visualize workflow. It features a drag and drop interface and an extensive image library.

Story Creation Apps

Android

StoryMaker 1 [free] provides a means of creating stories using templates and overlays, and the possibility of using audio, photos, or video.

Storehouse [free] allows users to share a collection of photos in a collage or album, or by telling a story that links the photos.

iOS

StoryKit [free] allows for the creation of an electronic storybook through the use of images, simple drawings, recording of sound, and by the addition of text.

Storyrobe [paid] makes photo-based slideshows with voice recording.

FotoBabble [free] adds audio to a photo to make a talking postcard.

Sock Puppets [free] lets users create lip-synced videos with characters. Various puppets, props, scenery, and backgrounds can be used.

Computer

Cartoon Story Maker 1.1 [free] is a simple program that creates 2D cartoon stories with conversations, dialogs (recorded and/or speech bubble), and various backgrounds.

StoryMaker [free/trial] is game-based software that asks for parts of speech (such as nouns, verbs, adjectives), and these are then inserted into a story with sometimes comical results. Educators can edit and customize aspects of the aspects of the program for their context. Backgrounds can be imported, but character templates are built in.

Web

Littlebirdtales [free] provides younger learners the ability to create digital storybooks.

Pixton [free/paid] is a visual writing tool that allows users to make a comic using images, clipart backgrounds and artwork, as well as speech bubbles.

Storynet.org [free] is a website that aims at connecting people to and through storytelling.

StoryJumper [free] allows users to create illustrated storybooks from scratch or from existing templates.

Video Editing

Android

VideoShow – Video Editor [free] is an all-in-one video editor and slideshow producer that provides music, themes, filters, emojis, as well as text input.

VidTrim [free] is a video editor and organizer that allows the trimming, editing, and saving of videos.

VivaVideo: Free Video Editor [free] is a comprehensive video editor and movie maker that facilitates the creation of video-based stories.

WeVideo [free] is a comprehensive and easy to use video editor that can mix images, text, video, and audio.

iOS

iMovie [paid] is video creation and editing software that can create easily shareable content.

Splice [free] is a video editor that adds music and effects to images and videos with narration. It includes access to free songs, sound effects, text overlays, transitions, filters, and various editing tools.

ReelDirector II [paid] is a full-featured video editing app.

WeVideo [free] is an easy to use and comprehensive video editor that can mix audio, images, text, and audio.

Computer

Windows Movie Maker [free] is a video editing software application that allows for narration, audio, images, and video to be mixed and edited with transitions and special effects.

Web

Video Toolbox [free] is an online video editing and conversion tool.

WeVideo [free] is a comprehensive and easy to use web-based video editor that can mix images, text, video, and audio together to form a compelling story.

Video Resources
Android

> *TED* [free] provides more than 2,000 TED talks from various people by topic and mood, and on a variety of topics.

> *Vimeo* [free] provides a variety of videos which are available across a wide variety of topics and genres, with users having the ability to upload their own content as well.

> *YouTube* [free] allows for editing and uploading of videos, where one can subscribe to various channels that offer a wide variety of videos on various topics and genres.

iOS

> *TED* [free] provides more than 2,000 TED talks from various people by topic and mood, and on a variety of topics.

> *Vimeo* [free] provides a variety of videos which are available across a wide variety of topics and genres. Users are able to upload their own content as well.

> *YouTube* [free] allows for editing and uploading of videos, where once can subscribe to various channels that offer a wide variety of videos on various topics and genres.

Computer – n/a
Web

> *Clipcanvas* [free] allows for the download of 600,000 royalty free HD and 4K video and film clips.

> *Mazwai* [free] maintains a collection of free to use HD video clips and footage, and some unique time-lapse and slow motion video footages that are

provided under the Creative Commons Attribution license if used commercially.

Motion Backgrounds for Free [free] is a place to download professional quality motion backgrounds and video footage.

Motion Elements [free] is a good source for premium stock videos, offering around 400 videos for free, as well as free After Effects templates.

Neo's Clip Archive [free] offers nearly 3,500 free video clips sorted by 25 categories free for use for personal, non-commercial purposes.

Pexels Videos [free] brings under one roof a video library of Creative Commons Zero licensed stock videos from a variety of different sources.

SaveTube [free] allows users to rip YouTube videos to their local computer in various audio or video-based formats.

Savevideo.me [free] allows users to rip videos from a variety of sites to their local computer.

TeacherTube [free] is an online resource that helps users to view and share videos, photos, audio, and documents on almost any topic.

Voice Assisted language Learning Resources (including Actions/Skills)
Alexa

Akinator [free] has a genie who will try to guess any character, real or fictional, by asking yes/no questions.

Magic Door [free] is an interactive adventure game that provides an original interactive story that spans various regions such as a castle, garden, forest, and the sea. The intent is to solve riddles, collect hidden items, and help magical creatures as you progress through the story.

Twenty Questions [free] is an Alexa Skill where the digital assistant will attempt to guess the animal-, vegetable-, mineral-, or music-related item you have chosen.

My African Safari [free] is an interactive adventure Skill for Alexa that takes users to Kruger National Park, providing a variety of experiences over two chapters, eight stories, and 26 possible endings.

Android

Google Translate [free] allows you to type or speak words or phrases that you would like to translate into other languages. It can also use the camera in devices to read the text of languages and provide real-time translations.

Sounds [free] is a mobile English pronunciation aid which helps in the study and practice of pronunciation using listening, reading, speaking, and writing.

Speakit: English Pronunciation Checker [free] shows how the speech sounds of American English are formed, and checks their pronunciation.

Computer – *n/a*

Google Assistant

Akinator [free] a genie will try to guess any character real or fictional by asking you yes/no questions).

English King [free] can teach English grammar, recite poetry, provide tongue twisters, and provide interesting facts about English.

Freeze Dance [free] plays music and stops it when it is time to freeze. A voice will then give you directions about which silly dance moves to make. This is only available in certain geographic locations.

Magic Door [free] is an interactive adventure game that provides an original interactive story that spans various regions such as a castle, garden, forest, and sea. The intent is to solve riddles, collect hidden items, and help magical creatures as you progress through the story.

Mystery Animal [free] is similar to Twenty-Questions where the assistant pretends to be an animal and users need to guess what animal it is by asking relevant questions. Questions need to be yes/no type ones, such as *'Do you have feathers?'*, *'Do you sleep at night?'* It can be played on Google Home or on the website.

Safari Mixer [free] uses Google Assistant voice prompts that ask what kind of body parts an animal has in order to create a new animal. An image of the animal is then sent to the user's phone, and the noise that new animal makes is played along with a fun fact about the animal.

Mixlab [free] allows users to create music by using voice-commands such as *'Play me a funky bass,'* or *'Add some jazz drums.'* It can be played on Google Home or on the website.

iOS

Google Translate [free] allows you to type or speak words or phrases that you would like to translate into other languages. It can also use the camera in devices to read the text of languages and provide real-time translations.

Sounds [free] is a mobile English pronunciation aid which helps in the study and practice of pronunciation using listening, reading, speaking, and writing.

Voice Pronunciation Checker [free] is an application that helps learners study the pronunciation, spelling and meaning of words, and provides a pronunciation checking mechanism through text-to-speech transcription.

Web

Dictation.io [free] is a website that uses Chrome to provide speech recognition for dictation. It helps you to write emails, documents, and essays using only your voice.

Ditty [free] is an Alexa Skill that will turn any spoken phrase or simple message into a musical ditty by matching it to popular music.

Dumpling the Pug [free] provides a voice-user interface to control the actions of a pug, and commands can be given in English or in Mandarin Chinese.

Forvo [free] is the largest pronunciation dictionary in the world. The aim of the website is to have a database of all the words from all the languages in the world pronounced by native speakers of those languages. You can type in a word to then hear how it is pronounced.

Google Translate [free] allows you to type or speak words or phrases that you would like to translate into other languages. It can also use the camera in devices to read the text of languages and provide real-time translations.

The Peanut Gallery [free] is a website where users can select short movies to subtitle with text produced from their speech.

WebQuests

Android – n/a
iOS – n/a
Computer – n/a
Web

Building a WebQuest [free] is a comprehensive overview of the template to follow when there is a need to construct a WebQuest.

Having Fun with Reading [free] is a WebQuest for college and adult level learners of English, where learners interact with texts and complete activities that promote cooperative and collaborative learning along with reading narrative comprehension skills.

Idioms in Your Pocket [free] is a WebQuest that is designed for high school and adult ESL students, and it allows them to discover the various meanings of English idioms.

OneStopEnglish WebQuests [free] provides a selection of WebQuests covering major holidays.

Pre-Writing Your WebQuest [free] provides prompts for users to complete in order to develop a WebQuest.

QuestGarden [free/paid] is a site designed by Bernie Dodge, the creator of WebQuests, for use by pre- and in-service teachers, professional developers, other educators, and those who work with them. The site provides hosting and template creation of WebQuests that then become searchable.

Using WebQuests to Teach English [free] is a WebQuest that can be used to teach teachers about WebQuests.

WebQuestDirect [free] is described as the world's largest searchable directory of WebQuest reviews.

WebQuest.Org [free] provides comprehensive information pertaining to the WebQuest model, and is run by Bernie Dodge, the creator of WebQuests.

Zunal [free/paid] is a site for educators to create, host, and then share their WebQuests with others.

Wikis
Android

EveryWiki: Wikipedia++ [free] aims to provide access to many wikis from a central application.

wikiHow [free] is the application associated with the leading how-to-guide wikiHow. It allows for searching of the wiki to find step-by-step instructions on how to complete almost any task.

iOS

Hack My Life – Life Hack Wiki [free] is an application that seeks to provide access to all possible life hacks. A life hack is a strategy or technique that can be used or adopted to allow for better time management or for getting more out of everyday activities.

Lyrically [free] offers access to a list of song lyrics curated by fans. Searches can be undertaken by track, artist, or by song, and there is support for in-app purchases.

Computer

DokuWiki [free] is a PHP based highly customizable and fully extensible wiki software platform. The advantage is that it requires no databases as all the data is stored in plain text, and for this reason, it is very popular and used by many sites. It has a variety of useful features, from locking to avoid edits through to a spam blacklist.

MediaWiki [free] is open-source and it is the wiki software used by Wikipedia. It is available in a number of languages, released under a general public license (GPL), and written in PHP: Hypertext Preprocessor (PHP) a server-side scripting language. There are many extensions and plugins available for free, including a what-you-see-is-what-you-get (WYSIWYG) editor.

Web

PBworks [free] (formerly PBwiki) is a real-time collaborative editing system with several solutions including one for educators. It offers a single workspace, where student accounts can be created without email addresses, and easy editing without the need for coding.

PmWiki [free] is a wiki tool that gives user-access control over individual pages, so they can be set for access by specific people with it being possible to set different passwords for each page. The software also allows for navigation trails through individual sections, insertion of tables, and provides a printable layout.

Wikidot [free] offers members the ability to create a wiki-based website with forums, where they can create a community, or publish and share documents and content.

Wikispaces [free] is a wiki hosting service that provides educators with a means to monitor student progress in real time and the ability to easily create projects and assign them to students, as well as editing tools and a social newsfeed.

Teacher Notes

Actions

_____

_____

_____

_____

_____

_____

_____

_____

_____

_____

_____

_____

_____

_____

_____

_____

_____

_____

_____

_____

_____

_____

_____

_____

_____

_____

_____

_____

_____

_____

_____

_____

Android

_____

_____

_____

_____

_____

_____

_____

_____

_____

_____

_____

_____

_____

_____

_____

_____

_____

_____

_____

_____

_____

_____

_____

_____

_____

_____

_____

iOS

Computer

_____
_____
_____
_____
_____
_____
_____
_____
_____
_____
_____
_____
_____
_____
_____
_____
_____
_____
_____
_____
_____
_____
_____
_____
_____
_____
_____
_____
_____

Skills

_____

_____

_____

_____

_____

_____

_____

_____

_____

_____

_____

_____

_____

_____

_____

_____

_____

_____

_____

_____

_____

_____

_____

_____

_____

_____

_____

_____

_____

_____

_____

_____

_____

Web

16
References

AbuShawar, B., & Atwell, E. (2015). ALICE Chatbot: Trials and Outputs. *Computación y Sistemas, 19,*(4), 625-632, https://doi.org/10.13053/CyS-19-4-2326

Alemi, M., Meghdari, A., & Ghazisaedy, M. (2015). The impact of social robotics on L2 Learners' anxiety and attitude in English vocabulary acquisition. *International Journal of Social Robotics, 7,* 523-535.

Alfa Tech. (2018). Google Assistant making a haircut appointment | Google IO 2018. Retrieved from https://www.youtube.com/watch?v=YCWJ0z6_z34

Bii, P., Too, J., & Mukwa, C. (2018). Teacher attitude towards use of chatbots in routine teaching. Universal Journal of Educational Research, 6(7), 1586-1597, https://doi.org/19.10.13189/ujer.2018.060719

Brown, D. (2014). *Principles of English language teaching,* 6th Ed. USA: Pearson Education.

Chapelle, (2005). Interactionist SLA theory in CALL research. In J. L. Egbert & G. N. Petrie (Eds.), *CALL research perspectives* (pp. 53-64). Mahwah, NJ: Lawrence Erlbaum.

Coniam, D. (2014). The linguistic accuracy of chatbots: usability from an ESL perspective. *Text & Talk*, *34*(5), 545-567, https://doi.org/10.11515/text- 2014-0018

Enge, E. (2018). Rating the smarts of the digital personal assistants in 2018. Stone Temple: Study Series. Retrieved from https://www.stone temple.com/digital-personal-assistants-study/#which_smartest

Dornyei, Z. (2018). Safe speaking environments – What? Why? How? *52nd IATEFL (International Association of Teachers of English as a Foreign Language) Conference*. April 10-13, Brighton, United Kingdom.

Facebook Business. (2018). Channel4: Humans. Retrieved from https://www.facebook.com/business/success/channel-4-humans

Fryer, L. (2006). Bots for language learning. *The Language Teacher, 30, 8*(33-34).

Fryer, L., & Nakao, K. (2009). Assessing chatbots for EFL learner use. IN JALT Conference Proceedings, PAC7 Shared Identities: Our Interweaving Threads, (pp, 849-857). Retrieved form http://jalt-publications.org/recentpdf/proc eedings/2008/E107.pdf

Fryer, L., Ainley, M. Thompson, A., Gibson, A., & Sherlock, Z. (2017). Stimulating and sustaining interest in a language course: An experimental comparison of chatbot and human task partners. *Computers in Human Behavior, 75*, 461-468, https://doi.org/10.1016/j.chb.2017.05.045

Kalantra, F., & Hashemian, M. (2018). A story-telling approach to teaching English to young EFL Iranian learners. *English Language Teaching, 9*(1), 221-234, https://doi.org/10.5539/elt.v9n1p221

Kim, N. (2017). Effects of different types of chatbots on EFL learners' speaking competence and learner perception. 비교문화연구 48, 223~252.

Levin-Goldberg, J. (2014). WebQuest 2.0: Best Practices for the 21st Century. *Journal of Instructional Research, 3*, 73-82.

Malewar, A. (2018). Lily: An incredible way to learn Chinese. Inceptive Mind. Retrieved from https://www.inceptivemind.com/lily-incredible-way-learn-chinese/4836

Marketing Charts. (2017). Amazon Echo & Commerce: 1 in 10 using their smart speakers to order products. Retrieved from https://www.marketingcharts.com/industries/retail-and-e-commerce-77252?utm_source=Marketing%20Charts%20Newsletter&utm_campaign=0414ef77c3-EMAIL_CAMPAIGN_2017_02_22&utm_medium=email&utm_term=0_77b507436c-0414ef77c3-15903393&mc_cid=0414ef77c3&mc_eid= d58e54c115

Meek, T. (2017). Better at listening, voice recognition will reshape your relationship with technology. Forbes. Retrieved from https://www.forbes.com/sites/samsungtv/2017/06/15/better-at-listening-voice-recognition-will-reshape-your-relationship-with-technology/#1d3e7ebd4148

Moussalli, S., & Cardoso, W. (2016). Are commercial 'personal robots' ready for language learning? Focus on second language speech. In S. Papadima-Sophocleous, L. Bradley & S. Thouesny (Eds), *CALL communities and culture – short papers from EuroCALL 2016* (pp. 325-329), https://doi.org/10.14705/rpent.2016.eurocall2016.583

Nordrum, A. (2017, January 04). CES 2017: the year of voice recognition. Retrieved from http://spectrum.ieee. org/tech-talk/consumer-electronics/gadgets/ces-2017-the-year-of-voice-recognition

Puentedura, R. (2006). Transformation, technology, and education. Retrieved from http://hippasus.com/resources/tte

Romero, P. (2017). Teaching and learning English through songs: a literature review. *MSU Working Papers in SLS, 8*, 40-45.

Sony Pictures Television. (December 14, 2010). IBM's Watsons computing system to challenge all time Henry Lambert Jeopardy! Champions. Retrieved from http://www.jeopardy.com/news/watson1x7ap4.php

Turing, A. (1950). Computing machinery and intelligence. *Mind, LIX,* 433-460, https://doi.org.10.1093/mind/LIX.236.433

UK Safer Internet Center. (2018). *7 in 10 children are using voice assisted technology finds new research from UKSIC partner childnet.* Retrieved from https://www.saferinternet.org.uk/blog/7-10-children-are-using-voice-assisted-technology-finds-new-research-uksic-partner-childnet

Underwood, J. (2017). Exploring AI language assistants with primary EFL students. In K. Borthwick, L. Bradley & S. Thouesny (Eds), *CALL in a climate of change: adapting to turbulent global conditions – short papers from EUROCALL 2017* (pp. 317-321).

Underwood, J. (2018). *Using voice and AI assistants for language learning*. British Council Teaching English Webinar. Retrieved from https://www.teachingenglish.org.uk/article/using-voice-ai-assistants-language-learning

Varol, O., Ferrara, E., David, C., Menczer, F., & Flammini, A. (2017). Online human-bot interactions: Detection, estimation, and characterization. *The 11ᵗʰ AAAI (Association for the Advancement of Artificial Intelligence) International Conference on Web and Social Media (ICWSM-17)*. May 15-18, Montreal, Canada.

Vygotsky, L. S. (1978). Tool and symbol in child development. In M. Cole, V. John-Steiner, S. Scribner, & E. Souberman (Eds.). Mind in Society: The development of higher psychological processes. Cambridge, Mass: Harvard University Press.

Welch, C. (2018). Google just gave a stunning demo of assistant making an actual phone call. The Verge. Retrieved from https://www.theverge.com/2018/5/8/17332070/google-assistant-makes-phone-call-demo-duplex-io-2018

Winkler, R., & Sollner, M. (2018). Unleashing the potential of chatbots in education: A state-of-the-art analysis. In: *Academy of Management Annual Meeting (AOM)*. Chicago, USA.

About the Book

In recent years, disruptive technologies have seen how our students interact with us as teachers change, and transformed how we as teachers prepare and provide learning opportunities. For teachers too, it may also lead to changes in terms of with 'whom' we will teach, and how best we might begin to integrate robots and AI-based digital assistants into the classroom as teaching aides or personal learning companions for students. Speaking to machines, and seeing or hearing appropriate responses actioned, provides learners with a reason to speak that is not contrived and one that is inherently motivating and meaningful. To this end, the pedagogical affordances offered by digital assistants are explored, along with the pedagogical theory behind their effective implementation with learners for the teaching of English to speakers of other languages (TESOL). The actions/skills best suited for use are covered, as are effective techniques for integrating them into the classroom. This is supported by tutorials for Action/Skills creation, photocopiable material, and a comprehensive list of resources. A means for evaluating the appropriateness and viability of Actions/Skills for enhancing language learning is also provided.

About the Author

David Kent is an Associate Professor in the Endicott College of International Studies at Woosong University. He provides teacher education through the TESOL-MALL graduate program where he currently serves as Head of Department. He has been working and teaching in Korea since 1995, and with a Doctorate of Education from Curtin University in Australia, he is a specialist in computer assisted language learning (CALL) and the teaching of English to speakers of other languages (TESOL). He has presented at international conferences, and serves on the editorial board of several journals. He has also widely published, from prestigious peer-reviewed journals, books, and book chapters, through to multimedia content and educational material in his area of expertise. Several of his books have been translated into other languages.

Also by David Kent

A Loanword Approach to the Teaching of
English as a Foreign Language in Korea:
Exploring the Effectiveness of a Multimedia Curriculum

Teaching with Technology:
Integrating Technology into the TESOL Classroom
Integrating the Internet into the TESOL Classroom

TESOL Strategy Guides
Digital Storytelling
The Prezi Presentation Paradigm
Podcasts and Screencasts
WebQuests
VoiceThreading
Blogs and Wikis

* 9 7 8 1 9 2 5 5 5 5 4 1 7 *